This book is to be r
the last date

B   re   KV-577-038

ISLL
T/E → Mt.pk

28. FEB. 1980   18 OCT 1990

28. FEB. 1980   13 OCT 1997

24. APR. 1980   19 OCT 1990

ISLL
H → FLC   28 JUN 1991
                     19 APR 1993   0 4 NOV 1997
20 M

21 NOV 1987
14 JAN 1988   14 MAY 1993
23 JAN 1988
1-2.88
29 FEB 1988   18 MAY 1993   06 APR 1998
29 MAR 1988   17 NOV 1998

331.257
WAL

HUMAN ASPECTS OF SHIFTWORK

Dr James Walker graduated from Aberdeen University with an MA. He then took a PhD in Psychology at University College, London, where he then went on to work for the Medical Research Council in its Industrial Psychology Research Unit on such topics as attitudes to factory work, sickness and other absences and shiftwork, etc. He then became Senior Lecturer at Glasgow University in the Department of Epidemiology and Preventive Medicine. He is now currently working in the Public Service.

He is joint author of *Staff Appraisal and Development* published by Allen & Unwin, 1976.

HUMAN ASPECTS OF SHIFTWORK

James Walker

Institute of Personnel Management
Central House, Upper Woburn Place
London WC1H 0HX

First published 1978
© *James Walker 1978*

Text set in 10/12 pt VIP Sabon, printed by photolithography,
and bound in Great Britain at The Pitman Press, Bath

ISBN 0 85292 165 9

CONTENTS

〇〇〇〇〇〇〇〇〇〇〇〇〇〇〇〇〇〇

AUTHOR'S PREFACE

∞∞∞∞∞∞∞∞∞∞∞∞∞∞∞∞∞∞∞∞∞∞∞∞∞∞∞∞∞

The purpose of this book is to bring to the notice of people in industry information from a variety of sources about the human aspects of shiftwork and to point to practical conclusions when this is warranted. The work is based partly on published material and research findings, although it is not a literature review, and partly on the experience of the author, who has conducted a number of field studies on shiftwork in different industries. These were carried out from the Medical Research Council's Industrial Psychology Research Unit at University College, London, and from the Department of Epidemiology and Preventive Medicine at the University of Glasgow. From 1968 to 1970 I was consultant to the National Board for Prices and Incomes on its shiftwork remit.

During the years I have been concerned with this subject I have benefited from the help of a great many people. To all of them I am grateful, but I would particularly like to thank my former colleagues Mrs G de la Mare and R Sergean. It is also always a delight to discuss the subject with A A I Wedderburn. My particular thanks are due to Miss Paddy Tenger for her careful preparation of the typescript.

The book was written on the suggestion of Dr R T Wilkinson of the Medical Research Council, Applied Psychology Unit. The Advisory Conciliation and Arbitration Service, and the Health and Safety Executive have kindly given advice. In recording appreciation for help received it should be made clear that no responsibility for the opinions expressed in this book rests on the people or organizations named.

Acknowledgements are due to the following for permission to quote from publications: The Controller of Her Majesty's Stationery Office; The Editor, *British Journal of Industrial Medicine*; The Editor, *Ergonomics*; The Gower Press; The Industrial Society; The Director, National Institute of Industrial Psychology.

CHAPTER 1

ၚၚၚၚၚၚၚၚၚၚၚၚၚ

Shiftwork: its nature and extent

INTRODUCTION

In one sense all the working members of the community are on shifts, only most people work a normal spell during the day and may be thought of as working a day shift in the morning and afternoon. An increasing number of people in modern society are working outside these hours which are considered normal, and are referred to as shiftworkers in contrast to day workers. In another sense shifts are taken to refer to the change of work-people between spells of work as in alternating or multiple shifts, for example the Oxford English Dictionary defines shifts as (a) relay or change of workmen or of horses; (b) the length of time during which such a set of men work. However, it is quite possible for someone to work unusual hours on a permanent or semi-permanent basis, eg nightwork, without exchanging shifts, and this is considered to be shiftworking. In the present book *shiftwork* (or *shiftworker*) will refer to the working of unusual hours outside those that are considered normal in the morning and afternoon, while a shift will refer to any continuous spell of work and will usually be named, eg morning, afternoon or night shift.

People have always worked at night or for unusual hours, including those who worked in service industries such as shops, catering or entertainment; or provided services such as transport workers or nurses or midwives; or served to protect the community and its property such as soldiers and sailors, watchmen, guards and gate-keepers. But the practice was unusual until the coming of industrial society. Nightwork in bookbinding shops in Britain had been documented as early as 1750, but it was not common and shiftworking in this country started for technological reasons in the iron and glass industries. In the iron industry it was the custom to work alternate 12 hour shifts, while in the glass industry alternate six hour shifts were worked. Some coal mines introduced shiftworking early: in textiles night work was tried and later abandoned, not to be resumed until much later (Bienefeld, 1972).

Generally, it might have been expected that as pressure for shortening the hours of work was successful shiftworking would increase and manufacturers would not be burdened with too high overheads. This was slow to come for a number of reasons but there has been a complete change in recent years, and particularly since the second world war, so that it is estimated that about one third of workers in manufacturing industry are on some form of shiftwork.

TYPES OF SHIFTWORK

It is possible to classify shift systems according to the most common forms that are worked. The classification may start with those shifts that are worked by day and then move onto shiftwork which involves nightwork, or it may deal with single shiftworking, then systems involving two shifts and finally three shiftworking. We may iden-tify:

Double day shift

Two shift working, usually of eight hours, is customarily worked by women from 06.00 to 14.00 and 14.00 to 22.00 although the times may vary, eg 07.00, 15.00 and 23.00. This enables the plant to be manned for 80 hours a week without a night shift, although meal-breaks, if they cannot be covered by spare staff, will lead to a reduction of the total hours worked to 75 or less. The shifts usually alternate every one or two weeks, but other arrangements are practical, such as changing shifts in mid-week or back-to-back working when the shifts are changed daily; the same crew are on the afternoon shift of one day and the following morning. The system lacks flexibility, from the point of view of management, as overtime can only be worked at the weekends and there is little opportunity for machine maintenance except at night.

Part time shifts

These may be worked at any time but are usually designed for married women and may consist of a short day shift in school hours or a short morning or afternoon shift. 'Twilight' shifts are popular in the evening (eg 17.00 to 21.00) after other members of the family have returned from work. In a normal week they add 20 hours production time but lead to administrative and supervision problems for management.

Split shifts

These too may be worked at any time and divide the hours of work into two or more spells during the day. They are used to meet operational needs, often in the service industries, such as transport. They are generally unpopular and attempts have been made to phase them out in some work, eg nursing.

3

Day and night shifts

An alternating day and night shift where two groups of work people alternate between days and nights, usually weekly or fortnightly. This is a very flexible shift system permitting overtime by both shifts and maintenance time between the shift changes: week-end work is also possible. The flexibility is of great benefit to management, but spending half his working time on nights and the constant shift change between day and night may lead to stress on the shiftworker. This shift system is favoured in Britain, unlike many other countries, particularly Eastern Europe where the double day shift system is more common. In comparing shiftworking in the UK, French, Belgian and German motor industries (Fishwick and Harling, 1974) it was found that double day shift predominates in the three continental countries but alternating day/night shifts in the UK. On day/night work the shifts need not be the same size, for the night shift may be a half, or third, or any fraction of the day shift with the amount of night work correspondingly reduced. The opportunity to vary the size of the night shift is another feature which adds to the flexibility of the system and enables variations in the demand for a product to be met.

Discontinuous three shift system

This is a system where, generally, three groups of men operate for a 24 hour period over five days and nights, eg 06.00 to 14.00, 14.00 to 22.00, 22.00 to 06.00. Shift changes may take place weekly or fortnightly or at shorter or longer intervals, similarly the starting and stopping times of the shifts may be varied. There is scope for flexibility as overtime shifts can be worked at week-ends, if more production is required, and maintenance can be carried out then. If this occurs the social advantage to the men of having every week-end free is curtailed.

4

Continuous three shift system

On this system the plant is operated round the clock seven days a week, without a break at week-ends. Four groups of men generally operate the system and changeover of shifts usually takes place weekly or more frequently. If the working week is 42 hours, the shift rotas are simple but if shorter hours are worked they become more complicated. Shift rotas, starting and stopping times and the choice of shifts are discussed for this and other systems in chapter 6.

Permanent night shift

This shift may be worked because of job demands as in the case of security guards but it is fairly common for fixed or permanent shifts to be a substitute for multiple ones. A fixed day and night shift may replace the alternating day and night shift. It is sometimes possible to recruit permanent night workers who like the shift for pecuniary or other reasons while those workers who find it difficult to tolerate night work may avoid it by working on the day shift. For management the fixed day and night shifts allow the same flexibility for overtime and varying the numbers on the shift as the alternating day and night shift. Sometimes a group of male permanent night-workers man machinery which is operated during the day by women on double day shift. This leads to problems of equal pay for equal work. There is now some relaxation of the legal limitations of permitting women to work at night.

Other arrangements

This classification of the different kinds of shift system is convenient and enables the numbers of work-people on the systems to be counted but it is also misleading and gives a distorted picture of the true situation. In practice surveys of industry (Sergean 1971, Industrial Society

1975) show that there is great variety in the kinds of shift systems and the arrangements which are made for working unusual hours. There are many different rotas for each system, with variety in the starting and stopping times of the shifts, their length and the arrangements for changing on multiple shifts. A few of the most common variations include:

the working of shifts of long duration including 12 hour shifts or even longer

the shortening of the working week

*the working of a longish period of shifts at a stretch without a break to provide extended periods of rest and leisure

*the frequent change of shifts between morning, afternoon and night shifts to allow some leisure at normal times every week

*the changing of shifts after, say, a month on nights to allow bodily adaptations to night work to occur etc.

These examples show that there is no particular rational arrangement in the pattern of shiftwork and contradictory solutions may be found to the same problem (*as in the starred items above), although the solutions adopted may suit the local conditions eg the type of work. In some industries and firms the patterns of shift hours have developed historically and may be due to custom and habit. There is scope in factories where shifts have been worked for many years to examine the shift arrangements to see if they need changing, either to improve their convenience for the shiftworker or to operate them more economically.

Sergean (1971) has commented on the variety of shift systems. 'Different kinds of shiftwork may bear little resemblance to each other in the extent to which they are accepted or resisted, in the administrative problems they present, and in the demands they make upon the worker.' He then goes on to ask what similarity is there between an alternating 12 hour day and night shift and a part time twilight shift or 'granny' shift. There are also great individual differences among shiftworkers who may include a young single woman on double day shift to a middle-aged married man with children working a continuous three shift system in a traditional shiftworking area. It therefore follows that generalizations about shiftwork and shiftworkers as a whole need to be treated with great care and can rarely be made. We need to know the shift system worked and who is manning the shifts, eg sex, age, marital status, for the problems in each case are quite different.

THE EXTENT OF SHIFTWORKING

No regular figures are collected of the number of employees on shiftwork but from time to time the Department of Employment has carried out a special survey or adapted its New Earnings Survey as was done for the National Board for Prices and Incomes (NBPI) study of shiftwork for 1968. The basis of the New Earnings Survey is different from the other two surveys both in its sampling frame of workers and in the industries covered, but there is a rough comparability. The manual adult (male and female) full time shiftworkers as a percentage of all such workers in certain industries were:-

Year	1954*	1964*	1968[1]
Percentáge	12.2	18.2	25.1
	*includes juveniles		

[1]It is not possible to arrive at the proportion of employees on shiftwork from other years of the New Earnings Survey. Although the surveys contain the percentage of employees

7

The results show that the proportion of manual workers on shiftwork rose from one in eight to one in four in the 14 years from 1954 to 1968.

It is also of interest to compare different industries in the manufacturing sector from the three surveys, and the results are shown in table 1.1. It is seen that the proportion of shiftworkers has increased in all industries but that the proportions are high in certain groups; namely metal manufacture, chemical and allied industries, engineering and electrical goods, vehicles and textiles. Among other industries not included in the table, mining and quarrying had 44 per cent of its workers on shifts and transport and communications 34 per cent of its workers in 1968.

Another way of looking at the numbers of workers on shiftwork is to tabulate the proportions (%) of shiftworkers on different shift systems; this is available for the two Ministry of Labour surveys but not for the Department of Employment New Earnings Survey. However a survey was made by the Industrial Society (1975) of its member firms known to employ workers on shifts. The basis of this last survey is, of course, quite different from the other two and the results are not even roughly comparable although they may be indicative. The proportion (%) of shiftworkers on the major systems is shown in table 1.2.

It is seen that three shiftworking (continuous and discontinuous) is most common followed by alternating day and night shifts, but that less than a fifth of shiftworkers

receiving shift and other premium payments, they do not take into account shiftworkers on day shift over the week surveyed who are not paid a premium, or certain groups like policemen who receive no premium. The survey therefore underestimates the numbers on shiftwork.

Table 1.1
Shiftworking in certain industries — the proportion (per cent) of manual adult (male and female) shiftworkers in three national surveys

Industry	New earnings Survey	Ministry of Labour Surveys*	
	Shiftworkers as a % of all workers		
	1968	1964	1954
Food, drink and tobacco	21.7	19.3	13.0
Chemicals and allied industries	35.7	28.6	24.1
Metal manufacture	50.1	43.5	41.7
Engineering and electrical goods	18.0	11.4	6.9
Shipbuilding and marine goods	17.7	4.8	2.5
Vehicles	38.3	32.9	12.9
Metal, goods not elsewhere specified	18.5	14.3	7.8
Textiles	24.8	22.0	11.1
Leather, leather goods and fur	5.8	2.9	1.1
Clothing and footwear	1.7	0.7	0.3
Bricks, pottery, glass, cement, etc	27.9	23.0	17.1
Timber, furniture, etc	3.6	1.5	0.8
Paper, printing and publishing	24.7	24.1	13.9
Other manufacturing industries	36.2	27.1	21.5
All manufacturing industries	24.9	20.0	12.5

*Includes juveniles

Adapted from *NBPI, Hours of Work, Overtime and Shiftwork*, Report No 161, Cmnd 4554 and Supplement Cmnd 4555–1 HMSO, 1970

Table 1.2

The proportion (%) of shiftworkers on different shift systems in the UK

Shift system	Industrial Society Surveys	Ministry of Labour Surveys	
	% of shiftworkers surveyed		
	1975	1964	1954
Three shift	45.6	41.2	47.4
Alternating day/ night	32.7	23.3	23.3
Regular night	3.9	11.6	9.4
Double day shift	12.6	16.7	15.4
Evening and others	5.3	7.2	5.4
Total number of shiftworkers surveyed (00. 0s)	126.6	1019.8	667.8

Adapted from the *Ministry of Labour Gazette*

are on double day shift. The three surveys further show that the systems involving night work were manned almost exclusively by men, the evening shifts almost exclusively by women and the double day shifts by both men and women.

COMPARISONS WITH OTHER COUNTRIES

The National Board for Prices and Incomes' (NBPI) report on *Hours of Work Overtime and Shiftworking* (1970) made an international comparison of the extent of shiftworking in the UK compared to other European countries. It concludes that there was no evidence of shiftworking being more common in other countries, and that in all of them there had been an increase in shiftworking similar to the UK in recent years. In a more up-to-date review of shift work (Maurice, 1975) further international comparisons are made. These are always difficult to do because the bases for collecting the figures differ and relate to different dates. The proportion of workers on shifts for all industry were '20 per cent in the UK in 1964; 21.4 per cent in France in 1963; 12 per cent in Switzerland in 1960; 22 per cent in the Netherlands in 1959 . . . In the United States it was estimated in 1964–65 that 24.3 per cent of the workers in the manufacturing industries were on shiftwork.'

It is also possible to make an international comparison of the prevalance of the different shift systems, so far as the figures allow. The scanty results show that three shift systems are commoner in France and the Netherlands, but two shift systems in the UK and Japan. One further comparison is of considerable significance, which is that on two shift systems the double day shift is the commonest form in both Western and Eastern Europe but in the UK the alternating day and night shift is the commonest form of two shiftworking. The two types of shiftworking are to some extent interchangeable and manufacturers and work-people have some choice as to which to adopt. The alternating day and night shift has been criticized by biological scientists who point to the stress it puts on the shiftworker's bodily systems, which is absent from the double day shift. The Trade Union Congress has also criticized day and night shift for the same reasons. This theme will be discussed further.

FURTHER EXTENSION OF SHIFTWORKING

In the medium term it is not possible to predict the likely proportion of workers on shiftwork. With the increase in automatically controlled plant it may be possible to sustain production outside normal day time hours with small numbers of staff monitoring the plant and a small standby maintenance force. However in the short term, whatever the longer term trends, there is little doubt that the numbers of shiftworkers will increase.

The shortening of the hours of work introduces another dimension into the problem. This reduction of the basic hours of work in recent years from 48 per week to 44 and through to 40 may have caused some of the increase in shiftworking for economic reasons. However the decrease in the basic hours of work was accompanied by extensive overtime working so that the reduction of the basic hours of work since the end of the war of manual workers has been more nominal than real. There are signs that this is changing and there has been some real reduction in the working week in the 1970s.

The pressure is beginning to mount for a further reduction in the hours of work and possibly for a four day week. Trade union leaders are starting to ask for a 36 hour working week. The increase in unemployment figures to a million and a half (1976) and the belief that some of this is structural unemployment contingent on the reorganization and modernization of industry in the UK provide powerful arguments for reducing the length of the working week. Further, if there is any success in containing or even dismantling part of the expensive bureaucracies in the public sector the pressure on available employment will increase. When these pressures result in further shortening of the working week it is probable that many manufacturers will not find it profitable to operate their plant for, say, only 36 hours in a week. It seems likely, therefore, that the outcome will be an increase in shiftworking in one form or another.

Another trend which is increasing the amount of shiftwork is its extension to certain kinds of office work. Even this stronghold of nine to five working has succumbed to unusual hours where computers are involved. The high capital costs of the computers and ancillary equipment, with the need to operate them for more than the normal daytime hours has meant that some computer operators and maintenance staff work shifts.

CHANGES IN THE HOURS WORKED

The operation of shiftworking in the UK must be seen against the general backgound of changes in the hours of work, for there is now much more flexibility in working hours than ever before. Here as in other areas of life there is increased turbulence. It is unlikely that shiftworkers will be content to soldier on in the same way when they see day workers enjoying the advantages of increased flexibility. Three trends may be identified: the working of much overtime; the introduction of flexible working hours; and changes in the length of the working week.

The weekly hours of work for manual workers in manufacturing industry was around 48 from some time after the war until the mid-sixties. It then fell slightly, but substantial amounts of overtime are being worked in the seventies as the following figures show.

Average weekly hours worked, full-time men
on manual work

April 1972	–	46.0
April 1973	–	46.7
April 1974	–	46.5
April 1975	–	45.5

The NBPI report gave some interesting figures on the length of shifts for the different kinds of shift systems in 1968.

These figures do not include all overtime worked, since extra overtime shifts at the weekend on discontinuous three shiftworking do not affect the figure of 8.7 hours

Shift system	Average length of shift in hours
Three shift continuous	8.2
Three shift discontinuous	8.7
Double day	8.4
*Alternating day/night	10.5
*Permanent nights	10.0

*Some four shift × 10 hours were being worked on the night shift but not to a significant extent in 1968.

above. Nevertheless, the figures are indicative as showing the amount of overtime on the shifts. There is not a great deal of scope for overtime on the three shift continuous system or double day shift except to cover for a relief who starts work late or to work an occasional double shift to cover for absentees. On the alternating day/night shift and permanent nights the situation is quite different and the report found that on the two shift system the average (median) length of shift for the day shift was nine hours, but for the night shift and permanent nights the average (median) length of shift was 11 hours. On these systems night shifts of 12 hours or over are very common; so the curious feature arises that the most arduous shifts worked, at night, are the longest. In general the pattern of hours worked is one of considerable overtime with hours of work on some shift systems showing the general pattern of overtime working but on other shift systems the hours of work are shorter and correspond more closely to the nominal hours.

Since 1971 in the UK, as in many other countries, large numbers of office workers have turned over to flexible working hours (see for instance Sloane, 1975a). Most readers will be familiar with the system. In principle all workers are present in the office for a core time from, say,

14

10.00 hours to 12.00 hours and 14.00 hours to 16.00 hours. They then can attend at any times from say, 08.00 to 10.00 hours and 16.00 to 18.00 hours arranging their times of arrival and departure in the flexible part of the day to suit their convenience. The lunch break is taken at any time from 12.00 to 14.00 hours, although often a compulsory minimum time of half-an-hour is laid down without necessarily setting a maximum time. The total hours worked over a period, often four weeks, must equal the nominal hours of work or on the settlement day at the end of the period any credit or debit hours, up to a certain number, are carried forward into the next four week period. There is often provision for staff to take up to a day off work, with permission, if they have built up sufficient credit, but rules may be made to prevent staff working a four day week. There are rules for overtime working and for counting sickness and other absence. On this system it is essential for the hours of work to be recorded and this may be accomplished either manually or on some form of automatic recording device. There are many variations to flexible working hours, mainly in the degree of flexibility that is built into the system.

Most shiftworkers cannot share in the working of flexible hours to a great extent. Some are excluded because the process demands continuous attendance. And for the rest, flexible working hours has not, with some few exceptions, been extended to shop floor workers, because of the difficulties of doing so. The work of production staff is often dependent on the process, on the machine or on other workers, so that the work demands attendance of all or nearly all and the operation of flexible working hours is impractical. Some flexibility of attendance is possible if arrangements are made between the members of different crews to exchange shifts to suit their convenience, for provided the process is manned the method of doing it can be flexible so long as a member of a crew does not work excessive hours. This opportunity for some flexibility by making arrangements between members of different crews is not greatly exploited and will be discussed further in chapter 6.

The reduction in the nominal length of the working week in terms of hours worked has been referred to, but another trend is a reduction in the number of working days in the week or a compressed working week. There was a fairly widespread adoption of a four day, 40 hour week in the US and Canada in the early seventies where the normal working day is extended from eight to 10 hours. These changes were largely at the instigation of management for a variety of reasons among which was the belief that productivity would improve, and that employee morale would increase leading to a decline in the amount of absenteeism and turnover. There are fewer start-ups and shut-downs on a four day week which could contribute to increased output. Some evidence has been collected which supports these hopes (Wheeler 1972, Hodges 1973) in surveys of companies which had adopted the practice. There was, however, a high failure rate in the US, up to 15 per cent, and the changeover to a four day week has slowed down. The reasons for this and the failure of the four day week to spread more extensively in the US after its highly publicized start are unknown.

In the UK there has been little attempt to restructure the working week into four days except among some smaller firms. One explanation that has been put forward is conservatism of management and trade unions (Churchill 1975) but there is no reason why this should be so when both have been quick to accept flexible working hours. The 10 hour day may be one reason, for it could lead to fatigue on some kinds of work, and the trade

16

unions are traditionally against the extension of the working day. When/if the working hours are reduced below 40 then the objection is invalid for the long day disappears and we may see a wider adoption of the four day week. There are other variations to the compressed week such as the four and a half day week or the nine day fortnight but they have found little acceptance here. The experience of the three day week during the fuel crises of 1972 and 1974 when in many instances productivity increased markedly might have encouraged employers and employees to have experimented with a compressed working week; but it is not, of course, possible to sustain permanently productivity which can be maintained for a short period, and the return to normal working after the three day week was universally welcomed.

In the UK it is on a night shift that most employees are found who work a compressed or four night shift week. On the changeover to the 40 hour week in the 1960s a number of companies, mainly in the engineering industry, found that their employees preferred to work a four night week and compelled the adoption of the arrangement against the wishes of the employers in some instances, and against the recommended five night week of the negotiated agreement. Other firms in the motor industry in Coventry had found the working of Friday night uneconomic because of absenteeism, and operated a four night system. Surveys in the engineering industry by the employers in 1965 and 1973 show that a substantial proportion of firms operate a four shift system at night. As early as 1960 the Confederation of Shipbuilding and Engineering Unions had, at their request, the national overtime and night shift agreement amended to allow for four or four and a half nights work weekly as well as the recommended five nights. However, the picture is not simple and reference to any survey which gives details of shift rotas found on alternating day and night shifts (eg Industrial Society 1975) shows that the rotas worked include four, four and a half and five shift working weeks and other systems which are more complex.

The compressed working week has, therefore, made an impact on night-shift on the alternating day/night system but has not as yet affected other shift systems. It is not possible to foresee what will happen in the future but a sudden and dramatic move to the four shift week cannot be ruled out of court. More detailed discussion of the compressed working week can be found in Sloane (1975b) and the well known book by Riva Poor (1970) *Four Days, 40 Hours.*

THE TRADE UNIONS AND SHIFTWORK

A further important change in the background against which shiftwork must be viewed is the extension of the trade union interest far outside their traditional rather narrow role. With the emphasis on participation at the workplace and industrial democracy in the company, work-people will not be willing to accept shiftwork, nor a change from one shift system to another unless they have been consulted. This goes beyond the customary negotiation of shiftwork premia and will take into account the total cost to the employee, including social costs, of working shifts. The TUC pamphlet on shiftwork and overtime (1973), which is a guide for negotiators, considers that all the arrangements for shiftwork should be negotiated with employers. The indications are that the procedures will go beyond consultation and that shiftwork will become the subject of negotiation and bargaining. Any general legislation which is introduced that strengthens the trade union position regarding collective bargaining will have its effect on negotiations over shiftwork and may compel the employers to take up a

18

bargaining position. At best there will be a joint management–union appraisal of the total situation within which shiftworking is to occur including shared access to the costing exercise which is a necessary precursor to the introduction of shiftwork.

The trade unions have been concerned about working excessive weekly hours and working excessive hours in one spell so that their interest extends over both the length and distribution of working hours. Thus the TUC (1973) acknowledges the need for occasional overtime on shiftwork but it does not favour the long hours of overtime which are associated with some shift systems such as the alternating day/night shift. Looking at shiftworking in a rather wider perspective any reduction in the weekly hours will lead to a reappraisal of the need for shiftworking, particularly the further introduction of two shiftworking. There will be considerable scope for experimentation and it is to be hoped that the trade unions will preserve a strong element of flexibility.

THE GENERAL PROBLEMS OF SHIFTWORK

This book is about the problems which management and work-people face when the times of working depart from normal day shift and some form of abnormal hours of work are adopted. When and how to introduce shiftwork, the arrangements to be made in the factory such as communication, supervision, etc are vital questions which have to be answered if effective working is to be maintained. But a large part of the book will also be concerned with the human problems of shiftwork for all areas of a shiftworker's life and of his family are affected. A few changes are for the better, for instance, he is financially better off than the day worker with the same weekly hours. There are other, sometimes surprising, advantages for those who adapt to shiftwork, but for the great majority of shift workers it is a cost, and if night work is involved a heavy one. There are physical effects of working unusual hours which submit the body to stress. The shiftworker's family life is altered, his social life is undoubtedly impaired and he may find himself isolated so that there is a general deterioration in the quality of his life. However it is important to realize that there are large individual differences in the adjustment to shiftwork and some can adapt and find compensating advantages. Whether a shiftworker does adapt or not is partly a matter of individual and family adjustment so what is tolerable to some is not to others.

✪✪✪✪✪✪✪✪✪✪✪✪

CHAPTER 2

Reasons for the introduction of shiftwork

Shiftwork is introduced in industry to secure a greater utilization of capital invested in plant and equipment, for the longer the equipment is operated during the year the more unit costs may decline. Whether this is so or not depends on a large number of factors which will be considered in this chapter. In the most general sense it will be profitable to adopt shiftwork if the increased return on capital exceeds by a sufficient margin the increased costs of shiftwork. The questions will arise of whether to introduce shiftwork and what form it should take. One way of viewing the problem is to consider the position at different stages in the development of the firm.

If a company is to invest in a new factory or a new process or plant, it is part of the investment decision to determine the number of hours the plant will be operated during the year, which will involve a costing exercise comparing day shiftworking with different types of shiftwork. Marris (1964) points out that it has not been at all clear in the past on what basis businessmen have decided the length of time a plant should be worked and it has appeared, sometimes, that the possibility of shiftworking has not even been considered. The costing alone is not sufficient, for many social conditions will have to be taken into account as well, in arriving at a decision to work shifts; for instance, the availability of labour, the attitude of the trade unions, the prevalence of shiftwork in the area, etc. Marris (1964) who is the recognized authority on the economic consequences of shiftwork did not believe that the benefits were sufficient to warrant a widespread change to shiftworking at that date.

In the case of a new factory the manufacturer can assemble the facts, make his decision and plan the plant from the beginning. The decision is not so clear-cut if the question is one of adopting shiftwork in an existing plant. Here the need may be to adopt shiftwork in part of the plant, in one department or only on one process. The costing exercise must be carried through but the employer may find difficulty in turning over from day work to shiftwork particularly if there has been much overtime worked. It will be necessary 'to buy out' the staff by protecting earnings if the change is to shiftwork without overtime: this can lead to much increased labour costs. There may be other established attitudes in the factory which makes the adoption of shiftwork more difficult and more costly. Observers have noted a trend in shiftworking in undertakings which start out with day work, then move to two shiftworking, then to discontinuous three shiftworking and finally to a full 24 hour coverage on continuous shiftwork: such a change has occurred in certain metal working plants. The move from one stage to the next will be taken in the light of the economic consequences but also taking into account social and attitudinal factors as well.

Another way of looking at the introduction of shiftwork is from the technological development of the industry. In some industries the technology determines that the process shall be operated 24 hours a day. This applies
22

to most furnaces as in iron and steel manufacture. A furnace or kiln may require continuous firing. In other continuous processes with gases, liquids or chemicals in which the materials flow in pipes and tubes, the technology demands continuous working. Even if the process can be temporarily closed or dampened down, the length of the starting and stopping times makes it impractical. In these kinds of industries, for example chemical, oil refining, metal making, the cost of the plant is often very large in relation to the labour costs, so that shiftworking is an economic as well as technological necessity.

In manufacturing industry the increasing cost of plant and equipment has also meant that in more cases it has become economic to work shifts. Machine obsolescence has become increasingly common where there is the possibility of the machine becoming technically out-of-date and uneconomic before its working life is complete. In this instance too, it may be economic to work shifts so that the machine's working life is extended by compressing it into a shorter period. Automation often leads to continuous working because of the cost of the equipment and the increased risk of obsolescence. In this connection the extension of shiftworking to office work has already been noted (Industrial Society, 1965, British Institute of Management, 1968). Where part of an existing plant is automated or expensive new machinery bought, the problem may arise of synchronizing the output of the new machinery with the old and achieving a balance, for the new machines may need to work shorter or longer periods than the old machines or processes which they service. A useful concept here is that of the indivisible unit which in any particular case is the smallest unit which can operate as a whole on a shiftwork basis.

A third way of looking at the need for shiftwork is not the capital cost of equipment 'per se' or the technological

23

need, but the level of demand. If there is an increase in demand leading to permanent new levels then a change to shiftwork may be the right solution. Or if by working shifts the costs and selling price of a unit of output can be reduced so that the demand for the product relative to its competitors is greater, there may be an orderly progression to multiple shiftwork. But manufacturing industry is only partly like this and the manufacturer is often faced with fluctuations in demand sometimes varying over the short term. The need is for flexibility in the level of output to meet the changing levels of demand. This case is often met by overtime working on daywork, but it may also be met by certain types of shiftwork which permit flexible manning. Alternating day and night shift, or a permanent day and night shift, permit the greatest flexibility in manning for the manufacturer; discontinuous three shiftworking and double-day shift allow for some flexibility with overtime shifts at the weekend, but continuous shiftwork permits little flexibility. Flexibility in manning where shifts are built-up by increasing the labour force to meet increased demand and then reducing the size of the labour force by effecting separations if the demand declines will be increasingly expensive owing to compensation payments and increasingly less acceptable. This may discourage manufacturers from adopting shifts unless they are almost certain that shifts will be on a permanent or semi-permanent basis. Flexibility obtained by working overtime on daywork or on shifts remains an option without the added risks of incurring separation payments.

STATED REASONS FOR ADOPTING SHIFTWORK

Two surveys included a question asking firms the reason for introducing shiftwork (Sergean 1971, Industrial Society 1975), the results of which are shown in table 2.1.

Table 2.1
The reasons for undertakings adopting shiftwork

Reasons for shiftworking	Industrial Society		Sergean
	No. of com-panies	% of total	No. of com-panies
Nature of the production process	80	58	27
Nature of customer demand	54	38	7
Cost of capital equipment	Not Classified	—	22
Maximum machine utilization from economic point of view	75	55	9
Maximum machine utilization from production point of view	82	59	29
Other reasons	20	14	—
Total no of companies	139*	100	Not known

*Some companies gave more than one reason.

From the Industrial Society, *Survey of Shiftworking Practices*, Survey No 94, 1975

The reasons for adopting shiftwork are connected with the nature of the process, the nature of customer demand, the economics of utilization and the need to meet production targets. These categories are largely self-explanatory. Thus the nature of the production process refers to undertakings such as iron and steel, chemicals or oil refining where continuity of working is essential. The nature of customer demand includes undertakings, often of a service nature, such as public utilities, where the demand is extended outside normal daytime hours. Maximum machine utilization from an economic point of view includes factories where shifts are adopted to increase utilization and reduce unit costs. Finally, maximum machine utilization from the point of view of production refers to those factories which work shifts because of limited capacity and to meet fluctuations in demand. In the Industrial Society's survey it is seen that 139 firms gave an average of just over two reasons each for adopting shiftwork. It is rarely that these are simple and those listed in the table must be seen as a group of overlapping reasons which determine the adoption of shiftwork.

Another view of the problem is to examine the reasons why firms which have once adopted shiftwork then abandon it, or have planned to introduce shiftwork but then fail to do so. The report of the National Board for Prices and Incomes (NBPI) (1970) provides the reasons shown in table 2.2 from their survey in selected establishments. The survey revealed that five per cent of establishments had abandoned shiftwork and two and a half per cent had dropped plans for shiftwork in the few years prior to the survey. The most common reasons for abandoning shiftwork or considering adopting it, but not doing so, are due to a fall in demand or other economic reasons. But a surprisingly large number of establishments gave reasons connected with the human factor, underlining the essential need for personnel planning as well as economic considerations and technical planning. The NBPI report goes on to add that:

Table 2.2
Reasons for abandoning or dropping plans for shiftwork

Reasons	% of establishments		
	Abandoned Shiftwork	Dropped plans for Shiftwork	All
Fall in demand for products	39	18	32
Uneconomic – for various reasons	23	24	24
Technical difficulty	13	4	10
Labour unobtainable	13	24	16
Employee dislike	10	28	16
Supervisory difficulties	10	8	9
Unions oppose	5	8	6
Absenteeism	3	2	3
Management – dislikes or considers unnecessary	1	0	1
Other	4	6	5

Adapted from NBPI, *Hours of Work, Overtime and Shiftwork*, Report No. 161, Cmnd 4554 and Supplement Cmnd 4555–1, HMSO, 1970

of those who have dropped plans for shiftwork, about 60 per cent give workers or union reactions or labour recruitment as the reason, compared to 28 who have abandoned shiftwork. This suggests that there are real difficulties involved but that once shiftworking is accepted a solution to the problems may well be found.

Thus labour difficulties are most acute when the change to shiftwork is taking place but as more than a quarter of the undertakings which abandoned shiftwork did so due to labour difficulties, the personnel function must pay continuous attention to the needs of shiftworkers including the problems of the supervisors and managers.

Shiftwork may be operated because of the technology of the industry or the nature of the service provided, but in manufacturing industry where the reasons for adoption are primarily economic there is often the option of deciding whether or not to work shifts. The following are a list of conditions which, if all or some of them are met, lead to a situation favouring the introduction of shiftwork. They are adapted from a discussion by Jones (1963) on the economic aspects of shiftwork, and Marris (1966):

The labour costs are relatively low as compared to the capital costs. The prime reason for introducing shiftwork is to increase capital utilization, producing overall a greater return on investment. The main (but not the only) increased cost is of wages. It therefore follows that if the capital costs are high relative to labour costs the need for shiftwork should be considered. A large part of the increase in shiftwork in manufacturing industry during recent years has been due to the increased capital cost of plant and equipment because of rapid technical development, greater mechanization and automation. All these changes have resulted in much higher productivity with reduced manning levels which result in lower cost of labour relative to the capital costs.

The expected rate of depreciation of the plant as the result of the introduction of new techniques is high. Obsolescence is depreciation with the passage of time. If machines and plant are likely to become out-of-date and uneconomic before their working life is complete then it may be profitable to increase utilization. The increasing speed with which a new plant is now replaced as technical

28

advances are made is another of the main factors leading to an increase in shiftwork.

The burden of taxation may be reduced by increasing the rate of capital depreciation. The type of depreciation of main concern here is wear and tear; that is depreciation with use. If a machine is worked twice as long in a given time period its useful life will be shortened and the rate of depreciation increased. It does not, of course, follow that doubling the utilization of the machine will necessarily double the wear and tear.

The adoption of shiftwork will make it possible to reduce costs. Certain prime costs do not increase in proportion to use. For instance the increase in the cost of land incurred by shiftwork will be nil and the increase in the cost of buildings will be slight, confined only to increased wear and tear. Further depreciation of plant may not be proportional to use, for wear and tear is not uniform over a machine's life: it may be slight in the early life of the machine, but greater in later life when there is the increased need for maintenance. Continuous use may sometimes increase the machine's life. Besides these savings in costs there may be others, such as stock economies or in heating the plant. It must be pointed out that expected economies in stock are not borne out for stocks of work in progress are usually to provide against fluctuations in supply of materials or work in progress, eg due to breakdowns, or in demand and these fluctuations may be unrelated to shiftwork.

A narrow range of products and a large unit of operation. One reason why shiftwork is not adopted is that the size of the factory is too small. The surveys of shiftwork such as that of NBPI (1970) have shown that shiftwork is much more likely in larger establishments. If the product range is narrow and the unit reasonably large it will be possible to achieve the economy of large scale production by investing in the latest equipment and increasing capital utilization by working shifts. In the NBPI survey more than four-fifths of establishments with numbers of staff greater than 1,000 employed shiftworkers, whereas only 16 per cent of establishments with less than 100 employees did so.

Undertakings with the advantage of being first to use a new technique or turn out a new product. A company first in the market either with a new product or with a new process which lowers the cost of an existing product will wish to exploit its advantage as extensively as possible. The company is likely to build up a market lead at least for some time. Under such conditions maximum utilization of the new machinery may be advisable.

The structure of the production process makes it possible to bring a machine or part of the process into production or take it out without substantial increase in costs. On continuous three shiftwork an opportunity for maintenance can only be made by stopping production, unless a machine can be taken out without closing down related processes. This is a condition which is becoming increasingly difficult to meet with the spread of automated lines and integrated plant. The tendency to keep low buffer stocks between processes to save costs also makes it difficult to take out part of the plant. If the plant is stopped due to breakdown, the practice is to carry out routine maintenance on other parts of the plant as well as the breakdown repairs, thus providing a flexible maintenance programme.

30

Supervisory functions are easily split-up. One of the management difficulties with shiftwork is the problem of communications between the shifts. If management is indivisible or apparently so, then operating a shift system becomes more difficult. It may be illustrated by the picture of the plant manager at home at night waiting for the telephone call to summon him to the factory. The difficulty recedes when it is recognized that it is necessary to provide supervision on the night shift and that the managers and supervisors have sufficient pecuniary incentive to work at night. In the past, and to some extent it is still true, the night shift has been inadequately covered by supervision and the shiftworkers left very much to their own devices. This is a false economy and provision of adequate supervision on the shifts is necessary: but it is also an added cost.

The average wage of shiftworkers is not too much greater than that of other workers. It has been mentioned that payments to staff in recompense for the inconvenience of working abnormal hours is the major increase in costs with the introduction of shiftwork. The increase in wages cost is made up of a number of items. There will be a straight premium payment for shiftwork in the form of allowances and/or additional overtime payment for weekend work (unless it is included in the premium) or by an increase in the basic rates. The actual hours worked may be less because it is customary to have paid meal breaks on some forms of shiftwork in certain industries and this may lead to a higher level of running costs. If the plant cannot be shut down for the annual holiday because of continuous working then additional staff may be required to cover for staggered holidays; although this may not be quite as costly as it seems for the staff are present to cover for increased sickness absence during the winter months. If the change to shiftwork is from day-work with overtime to no overtime, or similarly from two shift working with overtime to three shift working with little opportunity for overtime, then the workers will need to be 'bought out' so that their earnings are protected when they move onto the new arrangement of hours. Other workers in the plant who are not on shiftwork may still be able to negotiate an increase in wages either because of the risk that they might have to work shifts or because of the heightened level of wages in the plant. In general, shiftwork may add 25 per cent to the wages cost, although the NBPI report (1970) found that three shiftworking added some 30 per cent to the wages cost.

The average productivity of shiftworkers is not markedly lower than that of other workers. The evidence suggests that productivity on the night shift may be slightly lower than the day shift. But if excessively long hours are worked as seems to be common with some forms of shiftworking, productivity may fall further. There are other risks in that on certain tasks which require continuous attention and where men are working near their maximum capacity, the numbers of errors increase on the night shift particularly in the early hours of the morning. However it need not be assumed that the working of shifts, including a night shift, will necessarily lead to a fall in output, certainly not a drastic one. There are complicating factors such as fitter and generally younger men who can cope with any increased stress tend to work on shifts. This complex problem will be discussed in chapter 3.

The availability of manpower in the necessary quality and quantity. Before introducing shiftwork, management will wish to ascertain that the extra labour is available in sufficient numbers and with the appropriate skills. Certain geographical differences have been noticed in the willingness of workers to operate shift systems. In traditionally shiftworking areas, eg with coal mines or iron and steel works, it may not be too difficult to attract shiftworkers, for unusual hours have become part of the pattern of community life. In other parts of the country where shiftworking is unusual it may be resisted both by the workers themselves and by their families. It must be recognized however that availability of shiftworkers will be related to the general employment situation. It will also depend on striking a balance between the incentives to work shifts, eg pecuniary or any other such as shorter hours, and the deterrents including the physical, psychological and social disadvantages for the shiftworker and his family.

COSTING IMPLICATIONS

Management is interested in introducing shiftwork so that it may increase profits relative to the capital employed. Consequently a company contemplating introducing shiftwork for the first time or extending its existing use will instruct its accountants to prepare calculations comparing the return on different hours of plant utilization, which in effect means comparing the profitability of different shift systems. There are a number of ways of assessing the balance of economic advantages and disadvantages. One method is to determine which shift system will give the highest return on capital employed and another method is to determine which will yield the lowest cost of production per unit of output. Another approach is discounted cash flow. Examples of how to make the necessary calculations are given in Marris (1970) and Fishwick and Harling (1974).

Some of the main costs to be taken into account in the calculations are:

cost of plant and machinery, and including interest charges on capital

fixed capital costs including factory space

rate of depreciation with reference to obsolescence and wear and tear

labour costs of direct, maintenance and ancillary workers. These will include –

shiftwork premia and/or increase in basic rates

compensation for loss of overtime, if applicable

social security and holiday pay

cost of shift supervision and management

any effects of shiftwork on productivity or absenteeism

recruitment and training costs

provision of facilities on night shift, eg canteen, first aid.

Only a few of these are entirely or even mainly the concern of the accountant and he will need the assistance of his colleagues in line management and personnel if his estimates are to be more accurate than inspired guesses. For instance, the accountant is not particularly skilled in estimating the likely effects of shiftwork on productivity, absenteeism or wastage, nor is he competent to advise on the facilities that the company should provide for the nightworker. The accountant in calculating the gains and losses of different forms of shiftwork will need to be one of a team which evaluates the systems.

BENEFITS TO THE COUNTRY

So far the benefits and costs of shiftwork have been considered in relation to the individual undertaking but the extension of shiftwork will have wider effects on the country's economy. The main effect of the extension of

34

shiftwork is that it will increase the use of the country's capital stock. As such it will tend to contribute to the growth of the economy and, equally, a fast growing economy is one which is likely to make a better use of its capital. Alternatively the widespread use of shiftwork will also lead to a reduction in the country's capital stock for a given level of output, freeing the resources for other purposes. All the changes in industry which have made for larger units and the economies of large scale production, have contributed to the growth of shiftwork. Decreased working hours which make it unprofitable to operate only a short day shift have also contributed to the increase in shiftwork, and as hours of work are further reduced this will be decisive in encouraging further shiftwork. Many of the trends in modern industrial society point to the increase in shiftwork as a contribution to a growing economy.

A striking example of how capital utilization may vary is provided by Maurice (1975) who quotes the following figures of the average length of time of operation of a spindle in the textile industries of different countries in one year.

France	3920 hours a year
Belgium	4680 hours a year
Japan	4850 hours a year
US	6340 hours a year
India & Pakistan	6580 hours a year
Hong Kong	8544 hours a year

How far it is practical to increase the utilization of the country's wealth is not possible to say but there could certainly be an extension, sometimes in unexpected directions. In the case of certain public buildings and utilities a form of multi-purpose may be practised. For instance

35

schools may serve their main function during the day, but be used for adult education or community use in the evening. Similarly sporting facilities can be used throughout the day. At present however the community's capital stock is not employed in a very imaginative way and there is much room for development. A striking example is the opening of the expensive high street branches of the clearing banks for the minimum acceptable period. There is undoubtedly wide scope for the greater utilization of community resources.

Shiftwork may benefit the community in terms of creating employment, always assuming that there is a stock of labour available. If there is overmanning in an industry then the introduction of shiftwork will enable the workforce to be redistributed so that better use can be made of those who were formerly underemployed. The other case is of existing plant being worked on a single shift. If utilization is increased by working multiple shifts, then more jobs will become available. This will occur only if it is possible to dispose of the output at a price which will secure an adequate profit. Certain types of shiftworking may also bring into productive work women who find it impossible, for domestic reasons, to work normal hours.

If these are some of the economic benefits of shiftwork to the community, there are social costs to be set against them which affect the degree of acceptability of shiftwork. In terms of human welfare the costs to the individual shiftworker, and particularly the nightworker, may be heavy. The shiftworker may play an impoverished role in family life and in the wider social life of the community. The costs are not quantifiable and it is probably unrealistic to attempt to put a notional figure on them. They are very real and the next three chapters are concerned with these social costs.

CHAPTER 3

๏๏๏๏๏๏๏๏๏๏๏๏๏

Biological effects and performance

The biological effects of shiftwork occur when night work is involved. Work at abnormal times during the day may lead to inconvenience and disturbance to social life, but it has little or no physical effect, while with night work and the rotation between day and night shifts bodily habits are disturbed and there is an alteration of bodily rhythms. It is obvious that by working at night sleeping habits will have to be altered, meal times displaced and there may be effects on habits of elimination, but in addition to these changes there is disturbance to the circadian rhythms which follow the 24 hour day/night cycle. The term circadian ("circa" – about, "dies" – a day) is used, as the rhythms, if free running, are thought to have a periodicity of about a day.

A great number of bodily activities display rhythmicity ranging from cell division to the menstrual cycle but the rhythms which are known to be affected by shiftwork are those circadian rhythms which follow the periodicity of day and night or activity and rest. The body temperature, heart rate, blood pressure, ventilatory capacity and much visceral activity follow the cycle of day and night. Habits of elimination and more complex excretory rhythms such as the excretion of electrolytes in the urine also follow a circadian cycle. In general, activity is higher during the day reaching a peak sometime in the late afternoon or early evening and lower at night reaching a trough in the early hours of the morning. These rhythms in normal life coincide with wakefulness and sleep. An example of the 24 hour temperature cycle is shown in figure 3.1. The

Figure 3.1
A normal 24 hour body temperature curve

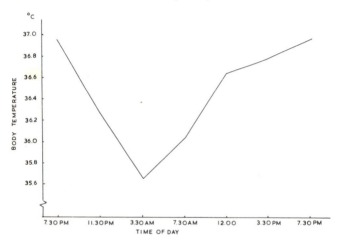

Adapted from Van Loon J H, *Diurnal Body Temperature Curves in Shiftworkers,* Ergonomics, 6, pp 267–273, 1963

temperature readings were taken for five days at four hourly intervals and the average obtained. It is seen that temperature is lowest at the 3.30 am reading and highest at the 7.30 pm reading. A characteristic of circadian rhythms such as temperature is that the old periodicities carry on into new routines so that if a man works at night and rests by day his circadian rhythm will persist at the old frequencies at least for a time until an adjustment takes place. The clearest example in modern life is the effects on East — West (or West — East) travellers who cross time zones by aeroplane. If the displacement of time is more than about four hours the travellers will feel the disturbance to their bodily functions, including the circadian rhythms which take time to adjust. If the inversion is complete or 180° it will take about a week for complete adaptation to take place, although some functions in some people, eg renal excretion, may take longer. Until adjustment has taken place the traveller is under some stress (jet lag). Politicians and businessmen are advised to be careful in their decision making which may be imperfect at these times. It has also been suggested (though not proven) that the effects on the air crew increase the probability of human error resulting in an accident. The traveller when he flies into the new time zone rapidly adopts the living and social habits of his new location and as a result his body readily adjusts. The position of the traveller moving across time zones is analogous to that of the shiftworker, although with him the problem of adjustment is much harder for, as we shall see, only some of his living and social habits change temporarily when he is on night work.

The next two sections explain the nature of circadian rhythms and the laboratory experiments designed to study their effects on performance. Discussion of their practical implications is resumed on page 50 to which the reader can turn if he wishes. There, consideration is given to bodily rhythms in relation to the design of the shift cycle, factory output at night, individual differences and accidents.

CIRCADIAN RHYTHMS

There is disagreement as to the degree to which the circadian rhythms are endogenous. It is sometimes argued that they are determined entirely by external events, others have suggested that they are similar to conditioned reflexes in that they are conditioned by outside agents, eg the light/dark cycle, but it is now generally believed that there are internal oscillators or physiological mechanisms analogous to internal clocks but that the degree to which the rhythm is endogenously determined depends on the particular function. The circadian rhythms are influenced by external events know as synchronizers or zeitgebers, in that the bodily rhythm becomes locked or entrained into the periodicity of the synchronizers. For humans the two most important synchronizers are thought to be the cycle of light and darkness and social habits, eg meal times, but there are secondary synchronizers such as the ambient temperature.

It is well worth while considering some of the characteristics of circadian rhythms in more detail for their disturbance can have a pervasive effect on shiftworkers.

1 *Phase shift* — This has been described in the reference to aeroplane travellers and the difficulty of their adjustment to changed time schedules. It is the basic biological difficulty which the nightworker has to overcome, as he goes to bed at about 8.00 am on returning home from work after the night shift, which transposes the time phase of his sleep by about nine hours.

2 *Frequency change* — Human circadian rhythms are synchronized to the 24 hour cycle but they may under abnormal conditions be synchronized to shorter or longer cycles. Thus Lobban (1960) lived with small groups of subjects in an isolated community in the arctic summer, and subjected them to abnormal time routines. The subjects' ordinary wrist watches were withdrawn and they were provided with watches which were adjusted so that they

recorded 12 hours in $10\frac{1}{2}$ or $13\frac{1}{2}$ real hours, thus establishing life on a 21 or 27 hour 'day'. Observations of certain bodily functions showed that the subjects' temperature rhythm synchronized on the new time scheduling after a short time and rapidly showed complete adaptation. Other functions such as the excretion of urine showed imperfect adaptation. Kleitman (1963) describes experiments which show that the temperature rhythm at least, is modifiable and can adapt to different frequencies, provided they do not depart too far from the 24 hour cycle. Attempts to adapt to 12 hour or 48 hour 'days' have not been successful, nor to watch systems of four hours on and four hours off.

3 *Removal of synchronizing stimuli* — The removal of synchronizing stimuli is possible for animals of certain species by having them live in conditions which allow the rhythms to become free running – conditions of continuous light or continuous dark. These show that the rhythms continue with a periodicity of about, but not exactly, 24 hours, so that over a period of time a phase shift takes place. With human subjects it is difficult to remove the external synchronizing agents as the endogenous rhythms become entrained to very weak signals. For instance it has been reported that a member of an Arctic expedition living under constant light always went to bed after making a radio call and that this may be enough to keep the sleep rhythm in synchrony. Some of the more interesting experiments in removing entraining agents or synchronizers is to have subjects live in underground caves or man made bunkers where the environment is as near constant as it is possible to make it. Establishing that the rhythms can become free running is a useful step in demonstrating that they are endogenous.

4 *Dissociation of rhythms* — By altering the diurnal cycle it is possible to show that some rhythms adjust more readily than others. Similarly if the cycle then reverts back to the normal 24 hours it is possible to observe when the different rhythms return to normal. For instance, in Lobban's experiment quoted above with men living on abnormal time routines of 21 and 27 hours, the temperature rhythm adapted quickly, the cycle of urinary excretion indifferently and the cycle of excretion of potassium in the urine was most resistant to change. This dissociation of rhythms would suggest that they are controlled by different oscillating mechanisms or 'physiological clocks' in the body.

5 *The master clock* — Is it reasonable to ask such questions as 'what are the physiological "clocks"? Is there a master "clock"? How are "clocks" coupled to synchronizers such as the 24 hour light/dark cycle?' Unfortunately very little is known and such suggestions as a master clock may be misconceived because the oscillators seem to be semi-autonomous, perhaps of a physiochemical nature. They may be locked together in a complex network which may be partly revealed by experiments such as those on the dissociation of rhythms.

6 *Individual differences* — There are wide individual differences in the ease with which circadian rhythms of different people adjust to new time routines. An amusing example is provided by the experiment of Kleitman (1963) in the Mammoth Cave in Kentucky. Kleitman who spent a lifetime investigating the sleep – wakefulness cycle, retired to the constant conditions of these caves with a colleague for a month and lived on an abnormal 28 hour routine comprising 19 hours of wakefulness and nine hours of sleep. Kleitman's colleague adapted comfortably to the new time routine but Kleitman, the 'guru'

of the subject, did not adapt and spent an uncomfortable and sleepless time when his hours of rest were out of phase with his temperature rhythm. Nearly all experimenters who use a number of subjects report individual differences in the rate of adaptation. The inability of people to adapt their circadian rhythms and habits such as sleep when they work at night may make shiftwork unacceptable to them.

The scientific study of circadian rhythms is a specialist subject which lies outside the scope of the present book, but reference may be made to the reviews of Conroy and Mills (1971) and Oatley and Goodwin (1971). As the latter point out, if we understood more about the effects of circadian rhythms and how to manipulate them, then there might well be opportunity for increases both in efficiency of work and the enjoyment of leisure, and certainly there would be important implications to shiftwork.

CIRCADIAN RHYTHMS AND PERFORMANCE

A question which needs answering is whether variations in circadian rhythms are reflected in the performance of people at work? As we shall see it is very difficult to tackle this question directly. It is theoretically possible to plot the output of factory workers and see if there is lower output on the night shift and if there is a dip in output in the early hours in the morning. In practice a dip in output in the small hours has only been shown on a very few occasions. There is the difficulty of relating output to individual efficiency in any real sense, for output often depends on machine efficiency, maintenance, fluctuations in the supply of materials, etc, which are unrelated to the operator's own efficiency. Factory workers as a rule work well below their maximum performance so that there is 'spare capacity' which they can call on if they should need

43

to, and this tends to mask any variation in their underlying efficiency. For all these reasons scientists are compelled to study the subject in the laboratory where they can control variables other than those they are studying more rigorously than it is possible to do in the field.

The circadian rhythm which has been studied most extensively in relation to performance is the temperature cycle. It has been used as an index of the sleep – wakefulness cycle. Kleitman (1963) in a series of early studies involving the normal waking hours of a number of subjects showed that on certain tasks performance varied with the temperature rhythm: when the body temperature was high later in the day efficiency was highest, and it was lowest early in the day when the body temperature was low. The kind of tests he used were card dealing, card sorting, mirror drawing, nonsense syllable copying, multiplication and simple and choice reaction time.

Demonstrating a relationship between body temperature and performance does not mean that the link is necessarily causal. One indication of the lack of a causal link is the 'post lunch dip' when, in the middle of the day, there is a drop in performance which is not paralleled by a dip in body temperature. Most people attribute the 'post lunch dip' to food intake, although this has not been proven, and it is accompanied by feelings of sleepiness. The relationship between body temperature and efficiency is more likely to be directly associated with a third concept – the level of arousal of the central nervous system. High arousal may be compared to alertness, low arousal to sleepiness. When arousal is low then performance is at a low level, but the converse is not true, for if arousal is very high performance may be low because the organism is over stimulated or excited and behaviour is disorganized; optimum performance occurs at moderate levels of arousal. This is a more satisfactory expla-

44

nation of the inverse relationship between body temperature and individual efficiency than suggesting a direct link.

Kleitman's early studies were restricted to observations made during the day, but there have now been a few laboratory and field studies which tested mental efficiency and measured body temperature when the subject slept during part of the day and worked at night. They may be thought of as simulated shiftwork studies of which three have been carried out by Colquhoun and his associates at the Medical Research Council's applied psychology unit. They promise to become classic studies in the subject and have been described by Colquhoun *et al* (1968a, 1968b, 1969), but there is a more general article which has a highly perceptive discussion of the problem (Colquhoun, 1971). Two experiments will be described of studies where the subjects altered their normal habits by working at night and sleeping by day, and in which performance measures of mental efficiency and measurements of body temperature were obtained. The questions which are of direct relevance to shiftwork are, firstly, did body temperatures adjust to the new routines and if so how long did they take? Secondly, was mental efficiency depressed by the change? Thirdly, do the measures correlate?

In Colquhoun's experiments, the first dealt with four hour watches mimicking naval watch keeping and the results are probably of more relevance to military personnel than industrial shiftworkers, but the second and third experiments dealt with eight hour and 12 hour systems which are extremely relevant to shiftworkers' experience. The second experiment with eight hour shifts will be described.

The first task used to measure performance was a vigilance test of auditory discrimination, that is dis-

tinguishing sounds which resembled certain sonar opera-
tions. The scores on the test were the number of signals
detected and the mean time to respond to the detected
signals. The second test was adding. The subjects were
supplied with sheets of printed pages, each containing
125 columns of five two digit numbers. They entered the
sum of each column at its foot and they were asked to
work as fast and accurately as possible.

The three eight hour shifts which were studied included
a night shift (22.00 – 06.00), a morning shift (04.00 –
12.00) and a day shift (08.00 – 16.00). There were two
tea-breaks and a meal break of one hour during the shifts.
The times of the shifts were selected in order to investigate night-time working and adaption to it, the effects of
very early rising at 03.00 (ie a phase-change in the work
rest cycle on the morning shift) and the correlation of
performance and temperature on a 'control' day shift.
Temperatures were read during the work shifts but in
addition they were read over the 24 hours on the day
before the 12 day trial, on the sixth day of the trial and
again on the 12th day of the trial. 31 naval ratings
completed the experiment. 11 subjects completed the day
routine; they slept from 23.00 to 06.30. 10 subjects
worked on the night shift and they slept from 08.00 to
15.30. 10 subjects who worked on the morning shift slept
officially from 19.30 to 03.00 but they tended to go to
bed later in the evening. Each of the four week periods on
each shift (separated by the breaks) were divided into two
consecutive sessions of 50 minutes. During the first
session the subjects carried out the vigilance test and
during the second they carried out the adding test.

The results showed that during the day shift body
temperature rose steadily. Vigilance detection rate
showed a close relationship to changes in body temperature, as did output on the calculation test which

46

followed the temperature curve except for the post lunch dip. The time taken to respond to the signals on the vigilance task also showed a relationship to body temperature: the time taken to respond to a signal was longer early in the shift when body temperature was low. To summarize, on the early morning shift the results were similar to the day shift, except that the temperature phase moved about an hour so that on the sixth day the temperature trough was at 04.00 coincident to when the shift started, rather than 05.00. Changes in the output figures showed a positive relationship to change in the body temperature but the relationship was imperfect. In particular output on some of the measures tended to decline towards the end of the shift suggesting that the subjects were fatigued by the end of the shift as a result of the early start and the short duration of sleep on the night before. On the night shift the temperature curve did not invert over the 12 days of the trial which means that there was *not* a complete adaptation: by the sixth day the body temperature curve had flattened and only showed a slight variation over the 24 hours. On the twelfth day adaptation had gone further but the curve was still flatter than a completely inverted rhythm would show. Examination of the scores on the tasks showed that performance was related to the temperature curve and it displayed some of the same flattening but on the whole 'performance adaptation' to the change in the times of waking and sleeping was more complete than with the temperature curve and in detecting signals the subjects actually improved their scores over the night shift towards the end of the experiment.

The second experiment (Hughes and Folkard, 1976) was carried out on six members of a 12 man British Antarctica Survey in South Georgia. At the season of the year when the study was carried out the light/dark cycle was 'normal' as sunrise was at 06.00 and sunset at 15.30. The

47

normal time routine of the six subjects was shifted eight hours so that they slept from 08.00 – 16.00 over a period of 10 days. On two days before the experiment started and on the last two days of the experiment four tests of performance were completed by the subjects at intervals during the day. A test of detecting tilted zeros in a matrix of normal zeros, a manual dexterity test of exchanging nuts and bolts and two tests involving medium memory load – a three minute test of verbal reasoning and a five minute test of arithmetic. Temperatures were obtained at four hourly intervals during the working day. The authors state:

> The conclusions in general are very similar to those based on studies where the subjects have not been members of a socially isolated community. Even after 10 successive days of an eight hour shift complete adaptation had not occurred in either temperature or visual search performance. Although the other performance measures showed no significant lack of adaptation, it is generally accepted that different rhythms adapt to a time shift at different rates and the adaptation of performance rhythm may well be quicker than that of a physiological one. The lack of complete adaptation could be due to the social influences of the six members of the camp who did not shift their routine and/or the opposing light/dark cycle.

The next four experiments will describe studies in the actual work situation where the tasks are real life situations rather than laboratory ones. Two describe the effects of night work on the temperature rhythm of workers and the other two examine the effects of nightwork on work requiring vigilance.

Utterback and Ludwig report (see Kleitman, 1963) an experiment in which a submarine crew, who normally worked four hours on and eight hours off, were required

48

to be on duty at fixed eight hour periods during the 24 hours. The work spell with rest periods lasted for 12 hours followed by 12 hours off. The temperature rhythm on the original system was required to adapt to two 12 hour routines of activity during the 24 hours and a certain imperfect adaptation did take place. But when the crews were stabilized on three fixed eight hour shifts three characteristic curves developed according to which hours the crew were working. Temperature was highest during the period of duty and lowest when the crew rested. The night crew had not inverted their temperature rhythms by the seventh day although there was a flattening of the curve. By the thirteenth day of the night shift, inversion was complete. In a factory experiment Van Loon (1963) measured the temperatures of three industrial workers over a period of 13 weeks on a five night week. The results showed that the temperature curves 'flattened' over the week of nightwork but there was not, in any true sense, an inversion of the rhythm. After the weekend break and at the end of the experiment the temperature curve snapped back to its normal rhythm so that the process of adaptation had to start again on the next week.

The following two experiments show that output can be affected by nightwork. Browne (1949) recorded the time teleprinter switchboard operators took to answer calls. The switchboards were manned 24 hours a day and the records were kept for a three month period. He found that performance in terms of time taken to answer a call improved steadily over the day shift until mid-day but then remained fairly constant to 17.00. Performance then fell off increasingly quickly until 04.00, there was then some improvement followed by a further fall at 08.00 hours. The results therefore showed that performance was least efficient in the early hours. A similar experiment was conducted by Bjerner *et al* (1955) who recorded all the errors which operators in a Swedish gas works made in reading from dials and instruments over a period of 20 – 30 years. Errors in recording reached their peak at about 03.00 hours. It is also worth noting that Meers (1975) has measured both temperatures and output of workers over a period on the night shift in two factory situations. The results showed some adaptation of temperature rhythms but it was imperfect and the adaptation disappeared after living one day in a normal routine. Output was somewhat lower on the night shift but this was caused mainly by organizational difficulties such as indifferent maintenance and lack of supervision.

FREQUENCY OF SHIFT CHANGES

These experiments give the flavour of the kind of work experimental scientists carry out in this area and point to some of their more important findings. What practical significance do they have for employers and work-people who have to organize shiftwork? Physiologists have been cautious about generalizing their results to the practice of shiftwork but some of them have suggested that a long period on the night shift or even permanent nights is preferable to a short spell, so that circadian rhythms can adapt. This may be true of submarine crews or members of expeditions in Antarctica but in the normal factory situation the position is not so clear cut. The circadian rhythms (specifically the temperature cycle) of factory workers do not adapt well on the night shift even over a long period of time: there is no inversion but a flattening of the temperature curve so that the normal bodily rhythms continue in a state of perturbation. The normal factory worker has two days off every week when his living habits return to daytime routines with the result that the temperature rhythms revert immediately to their normal pattern so that the adaptive process has to start again on the next week. Shiftworkers at night often cling to their day-time habits as best they can so that, for instance, the social Zeitgebers tend to hold the circadian rhythms in their normal periodicities, and full adaptation becomes impossible. It may be that there is long term adaptation to shiftwork, which means that the period before 'flattening' starts is shorter on the night shift week with workers who have had long experience of shiftwork. For example, with the experienced shiftworker 'flattening' of the temperature curve may occur on the second or third night of the week while with the tyro 'flattening' may not occur until the fifth night. There is some evidence for the long term effect, but readaptation still has to take place after the weekly break.

Other experts doubt the validity of the arguments for a long period on the night shift and are attracted to the case for operating rapidly rotating systems. These shift systems involve changing shifts after a spell of two or three nights. In this case there is no question of adjustment of the circadian cycle and there is probably little disturbance to the rhythms after only two nights. Some shiftworkers complain that fatigue builds up over the period of a week on nights but if only two night shifts are worked in sequence this is less inclined to happen. It is therefore argued that it is better to get the night shift over in a short burst, even though the circadian rhythms remain on the normal daytime cycle and work is being carried out under some stress.

The pros and cons of permanent night work and rapidly rotating shifts are discussed in a wider context in chapter 6. As Hughes and Folkard remark:

expert opinion as to the optimum form of shift systems is divided, however, between those who favour 'permanent' systems and those who favour rapidly rotating ones.

51

OUTPUT ON THE NIGHT SHIFT

The second practical question is how important is the experimentalists' demonstration that mental efficiency declines on the night shift? What does it mean in terms of factory output? It must be noted that even in some experiments the decrease in output at night does not always occur. Allusi (1972) has shown that subjects working on a four hour on, four hours off schedule can keep up a constant output for long periods of time in a simulated aerospace cabin. The effects of diurnal variation became apparent when the crews were overloaded or stressed by, for instance, lack of sleep. Allusi gave his subjects interesting and meaningful tasks which contrasts with some experimenters where the tasks have been trivial. It is also noteworthy that the tasks which have shown a decreased performance at night usually involve vigilance and sustained attention and much experimental evidence has shown that performance on work which requires constant attention is sensitive to adverse conditions.

In the usual factory situation there is no evidence that output is substantially less on the night shift. In the First World War the Health of Munitions Workers Committee (1917) examined output on the day shift and the night shift and found that it was about the same or only slightly less on the night shift, although working a permanent night shift for a long time did result in lower output. Wyatt and Marriott (1953) during and just after the Second World War, similarly found little difference between output on the day shift and the night shift in a variety of factory situations, although output might be slightly less, in the order of five per cent less at night compared to output during the day. Both the wartime studies showed that on alternating day/night shifts, which changed fortnightly or monthly, output was high in the

52

first week of the night shift and declined in subsequent weeks which suggested there was an accumulation of fatigue over the night shift. Conversely on the first week of the day shift output was low but increased in subsequent weeks which suggested that fatigue from the night shift was being gradually dissipated over a period of days. These results were obtained under conditions of work which were in general much more arduous than those of today. More up-to-date information, which yields a very similar picture, is provided by the National Board for Prices and Incomes (1971). They asked the establishments surveyed to compare productivity on the night shift compared to the day shift. They further sub-divided their sample into establishments which had made measured comparisons, about a third of them, and those whose comparisons were based on impressions and experience. The results are shown in table 3.1. Seventy-

Table 3.1

Comparison of productivity as between day and night shifts (for similar work)

Productivity on night shift as compared to day shift for firms making quantitative assessments	Per cent of establishments which had:	
	made comparative measurements	not made comparative measurements
Much less	3	2
Slightly less	36	20
The same	58	71
More	13	7

Adapted from NBPI, *Hours of Work, Overtime and Shiftwork*, Report No 161, Cmnd 4554 and supplement Cmnd 4555 – 1, 1970

two per cent of the establishments which had taken measurements said that productivity was the same or more on the night shift; nearly all the remainder said productivity was only slightly less. Firms which had not made measurements but relied on experience gave figures which were similar.

It thus seems that companies may expect that productivity on the night shift will be about the same or slightly less than on the day shift. In very few cases will productivity be much less. It does not of course follow that the differences in efficiency between the night shift and the day shift are mainly related to human efficiency: it is much more probable that any difference can be attributable primarily to organizational differences. For instance, in the survey quoted 13 per cent of establishments found higher efficiency on the night shift. The cause of this is likely to be the uninterrupted runs which are possible on the night shift due to a lack of stoppages, which may be a feature of the day shift. Indeed the night shift sometimes operates too long without the necessary maintenance. Similarly the reasons for the 'slightly' less and 'much' less productivity found in some establishments on the night shift are likely to be due to such factors as the lack of adequate supervision and the difficulties which follow. It is the organizational factors which are paramount, but management should not ignore the possibility that some of the difference is due to the human factor.

The kind of decrement in mental performance which the scientists have demonstrated to occur at night in the factory situation, might result not so much in a reduction of output but in an occasional error due to a slowness to respond or a failure to notice a signal. Events of this sort could lead to an accident (although the evidence discussed later is inconclusive), it could lead to a breakdown in a machine and it might, given a particular set of circumstances, lead to a catastrophe, eg error by an air traffic controller. Management can analyse the jobs which workers have to perform in the middle of the night and in the small hours to see if they are the kind where output falls or errors occur as a result of circadian variation or loss of sleep. On critically important or hazardous jobs management can take action. If such a job requires constant attention or vigilance then steps can be taken to avoid the falls in performance and the probability of error. One way is to allow adequate rest periods as it has been found that the interpolation of a rest period at the point before the decline in output occurs can avert it. Another possibility, although an expensive one, is to provide relief operators and this may be desirable in the middle of the night shift on certain types of continuous work. Yet another possibility is to arrange for an exchange of jobs, for this can act very like a rest period in preventing dips in performance. Attention should also be paid to the operator's motivation and attempts made to avoid designing jobs which are so trivial in their execution that no worker can maintain an interest. Whatever the solution adopted it should only be after a thorough examination of the particular job.

Factory conditions are quite different during the day than at night and it is difficult to make comparisons between the performance of day workers and shiftworkers. The two groups are usually on different kinds of work so that comparisons are not possible and it is also relatively uncommon to be able to record output on an hourly basis. Further, the shiftworkers are selected men in that those who are unfit or otherwise unsuited for shiftwork are not selected or leave shiftworking voluntarily. In comparing the efficiency of day workers and shiftworkers, like is not being compared with like so that the comparisons become meaningless. The variety of material factors affecting factory output

> usually entirely swamp any physiological changes in performance, such as can be demonstrated in the laboratory, or occasionally under particularly favourable circumstances where the workshop can be made to approximate closely to the laboratory conditions (Browne, 1949).

Ray *et al* (1961) carried out an extensive survey of the literature of human performance in relation to the work — rest cycle and concluded that output was relatively unaffected. It is perhaps only on the type of tasks discussed which involve vigilance and sustained attention that effects of human decrement in performance become noticeable as a result of shiftwork.

INDIVIDUAL DIFFERENCES

A substantial number of shiftworkers, when asked, state that they prefer shiftwork to day work while others, if they had the choice, would prefer to change to day work. The question may be an unreal one, for the shiftworker often could not find a job with comparable pay on day work. The question which should be asked is 'if you were offered a job on daywork with the same pay and conditions as your shiftwork job, which would you choose?' Nevertheless all the attitude surveys show individual differences in adjustment to shiftwork, some workers settling down well and others barely tolerating it. Thiis-Evansen (1970) writes that about 20 per cent of workers are not able to tolerate shiftwork and have to move to other work. There is no way of detecting these people beforehand, instead they start nightwork and find that over a period of a few months it is physically intolerable and they move back to daywork. A great step forward would be taken if it were possible to identify workers who were unsuitable for shiftwork before they started it, so that they could be advised not to take it up. Some people get 'trapped' in the shiftworking situation because of the high wages even though they dislike nightwork. It is, of course, most unlikely that all people are divided into those who can adjust to nightwork and those who cannot. Probably a minority 20 per cent can never adjust, a minority of about the same size would adjust quite well and the members of the remaining population lie between the two extremes.

Individual differences in adjustment to shiftworking have not been studied at all thoroughly but a few tentative steps have been taken. It is a matter of everyday observation that there are 'morning types' and 'evening types'. Those who are 'morning types' are alert during the early part of the day, work at their best then, but feel drowsy and lethargic in the evening. For the 'evening types' the converse holds. Kleitman (1963) indentified the two types of student, distinguishing between those who liked to study in the late evening and sleep late the following morning and those who liked to rise early to study having retired early the night before. Kleitman found that the temperature peak of the 'morning types' occurred earlier in the day than the temperature peak of the 'evening types'.

The work was taken a step further by Blake (1971) who showed that the body temperature of introverts was higher than extroverts earlier in the day and the temperature of extroverts was higher later in the day. Measurement of introversion was by means of a personality test. The introvert, it will be recalled, tends to be inward looking and to withdraw from social situations, while the extrovert is outward looking, talkative and active at making social contacts. Blake next tested a large number

57

of subjects at different times of the day on a variety of tasks and at the same time measured the subjects' temperatures. He also got them to complete the introversion/extroversion test. He then correlated the different measures for each time of the day that they were recorded. The kind of tasks were similar to those used by Colquhoun, eg a letter cancellation test, vigilance detection of an occasional slight difference in the duration of a regularly repeated short tone, calculations, various measures of reaction time, etc. The results with the letter cancellation test were as follows. At 08.00 the correlation between introversion and temperature was +0.38, at 21.00 hours the correlation was −0.43 showing quite clearly that in the morning the introverts' temperatures were higher, while in the evening the body temperatures of the extroverts were higher. Next the measures of introversion and temperature were correlated with the measures of output on the cancellation task at different times of the day. With errors in cancelling there was no significant relation with temperature; but at 08.00 hours introversion was correlated with quantity of output +0.42 and at 21.00 hours the correlation was −0.28 (not significant). These results showed that quantity of output on the cancellation task was higher for introverts than extroverts in the morning, but tended to be higher for extroverts in the evening. In the other experiments the relation between introversion and temperature rhythm held good, but the relationship between introversion and performance at different times of the day was imperfect; indeed on one task the relationship was reversed. Blake goes on to argue that the relationships are due to different levels of arousal or 'sleepiness'. Introverts have a higher level of arousal than extroverts in the morning, for both groups a rise occurs thoughout the day but more quickly for extroverts so that in the evening they are more alert. It may be that introverts tend to be the 'morning types' and extroverts the 'evening types'. Whether individual differences in personality are related to the facility for adjusting to shiftwork remains to be fully explored. The results of one study do lend support to this suggestion for Nachreiner (1975) found that shiftworkers who were rather introverted and tended to be emotionally unstable had difficulty in adjusting to shiftwork and many of them would like to transfer to daywork.

One of the few studies of individual differences of shiftworkers was made by Ostberg (1973). His subjects were computer operators and output handlers on a three shift discontinuous system. The investigator devised a questionnaire which would sort out his subjects into 'morning' and 'evening' types. The questionnaire asked such questions as:–

Do you experience difficulties in getting out of bed when you wake up in the morning?
(a) very often; (b) sometimes; (c) seldom; (d) very seldom

If you were free to choose at what time would you go to bed at night?
(a) after 01.00; (b) between 23.30 and 01.00; (c) between 22.00 and 23.30; (d) before 22.00

On the basis of the answers to the questionnaire the computer staff were divided into a 'morning' group, an 'evening' group and an intermediate group. The 'morning' group experienced most interference to their sleep when they were on the night shift and slept best when they were on the morning shift. The 'evening' group slept best after the afternoon shift. Ostberg also collected records of food intake and made tests of fitness. The general conclusions were that the evening types had the least difficulty in adapting to the shift schedules, that the morning types had the most difficulty, and the middle types adapted in an intermediate way. In another study Ostberg and Svensson (1975) have shown that it is important to take into account individual differences between shiftworkers when examining output requiring physical effort. They suggested that shiftworkers who do not adapt well to night work, behave as though they were 'functionally' older than those who do adapt well.

The work on individual differences in the adaptation to shiftwork has not progressed very far, but it is urgent that more research should be carried out as it would be of real benefit if tests of adaptability to shiftwork could be devised. These could be applied before workers went on to shifts involving night work. It is argued in chapter 6 that there is probably no ideal or optimum arrangement of shift rotas but that the best arrangement is to preserve flexibility so that the worker can select the hours of work which suit him best. For instance, some firms with a permanent night shift have no difficulty in recruiting willing night workers and there are cases recorded of waiting lists for the night shift. The largest pay off in relation to expenditure would be a determined effort to examine individual differences of shiftworkers. In the meantime the manager, while he has to ensure that shifts are manned, can extend recognition of the fact that there are people who find it very difficult to adjust physically to night work and some who find it impossible.

ACCIDENTS

The studies on accidents in relation to shiftwork, have been reviewed by Menzel (1962). The results are not in agreement and he quotes a number of investigations which show no association between the number of accidents and nightwork, including one where proportionately more accidents occurred on the afternoon shift.

60

Andlauer and Fourré (1962) studied accidents in five undertakings, two mines and three works in the steel industry. In all five accident rates on the night shift were less than on the other two shifts. When however the very serious accidents were separated, those involving a loss of working time of more than 15 days or partial or total incapacity, it was found that more of these occurred at night. If this is generally the case then deaths from accidents might be expected to be greater among shift-workers than day workers, but a study of mortality among the two groups (Taylor and Pocock, 1972) did not demonstrate any relationship in the number of deaths through accident.

Two British studies have been carried out. Vernon (1940) described an early investigation in which accidents at different times of the shifts were tabulated and they tended to be high at the beginning of the night shift. He associated this with the excited state in which men came to work after an evening's social activity. Wyatt and Marriott (1953) analysed the accident records of 13,962 men in five factories. In each factory accidents were slightly higher on the night shift but the differences were not significant. They showed no trends in hourly varia-tion. The investigators point out that for minor injuries men are less likely to go to the ambulance room at nights, particularly if it involves a walk in the dark some distance from the factory floor.

The results are inconclusive and do not answer the question whether nightwork is associated with accidents, but they do suggest that any relationship cannot be very definite. In so far as accidents are associated with human performance, and human error is a feature of most accidents, then it might be expected that the accident rate in factories would be higher in the middle of the night shift than at other times. Fatigue is greatest in the early hours and the metabolism at its lowest, but there is no evidence of increased accidents then. Just as it is difficult to compare output on the day shift and the night shift, so it is difficult to compare accidents. There is generally much more activity in a factory by day, and it may be that the risk of accidents is higher than at night. Wyatt and Marriott write:

> In the present state of our knowledge any attempt to explain the causes of the hourly and daily variations in accident frequency would be largely guesswork.

That was 25 years ago but the same is essentially true today.

An overview

A review article with an international flavour by three experts in the experimental field, Rutenfranz, Knauth and Colquhoun (1976) has brought together the main findings which the authors believe are sufficiently authoritative to provide a basis for advice to management. They are:

single night shifts are better than consecutive night shifts . . .

at least 24 hours free time should be allowed after each night shift . . .

the cycle of a shift system should not be too long

it is better to have a short cycle, eg four weeks, and a regular system of rotation because the planning of the social life is easier for the workers and their families

the length of the shift should be related to the type of work

normally the length of the shift should not exceed eight hours. Only in special cases if the work is light, referring to the physical energy expenditure and the mental load, the shift may be extended to 12 hours in connection with continuous shiftwork as many free weekends as possible should be arranged. . . .

The recommendations or as they are called 'criteria for optimal shift schedules' leave many questions unanswered and some of the criteria, such as the desirability of leaving as many free weekends as possible do not rest on experimental evidence, but a start has been made. The work would proceed at a greater pace if the experimentalists could find factory facilities for conducting their work. At present they tend to work in the laboratory, to make *ad hoc* observations in the field, or to wait for changes to occur in the normal way, the effects of which they can then observe. What is needed is a far-sighted employer and work force who would be willing to carry out experimental changes on shift arrangements. Nevertheless progress has been made and the scientist may in time be able to put forward guidelines. The author believes that much might be achieved by a more thorough study of individual differences in adaptation to shiftwork.

CHAPTER 4

Shiftwork and health

Night work is often spoken of as unnatural. It may be accompanied by feelings of fatigue, by loss of appetite and indigestion, and difficulties in sleeping. One study showed that 43 per cent of shiftworkers took patent medicines every day or several times a week. Shiftworkers themselves often blame their hours of work for causing ill health and the belief that shiftwork (specifically night work) affects health is prevalent. Accordingly industrial medical officers and others have devoted quite a lot of effort to finding out if the belief is valid.

Shiftworkers do not appear to die earlier as a result of the hours they work. Taylor and Pocock (1972) carried out a study of mortality among 8,603 men in ten industrial undertakings over a 12 year period. The sample consisted of all manual workers in the organizations who had completed 10 years service between 1946 and 1968. The men were divided into day workers, those who had completed at least 10 years on shiftwork and ex-shiftworkers. Account was also taken of the type of shift system the men worked on. There were no significant differences in mortality rates between the three groups, and the rates were very close to the expected number of deaths derived from national rates. There was a small non-significant but consistent tendency for ex-shiftworkers to have higher mortality. It can be argued that shiftworkers and dayworkers are not on the same type of work and therefore the comparison is invalid. Fortunately it was possible to compare maintenance workers on daywork and shiftwork, but there were no differences in mortality which could be attributed to shiftwork. Similarly when the causes of death were examined none were associated in a convincing way with shiftwork. This study at present provides the definitive answer that there is no relation between working on shifts and mortality.

SHIFTWORK AND ABSENCE

If shiftworking affected mortality rates this would be a gross effect and is probably not to be expected. A more sensitive measure is sickness and other absence which have been shown to be affected by the hours of work in other contexts. For instance the early work of the Health of Munitions Workers Committee (1918) showed that there was proportionately more absence when the hours of work were long, than when they were of a more moderate length. Similar observations were made during the Second World War. The relationship has not been demonstrated recently, as the hours of work are much shorter now than in the earlier times of emergency and the physical effort of work has generally decreased. There have been numerous studies testing for a relationship between shiftwork and absence. The early research reviewed by Andlauer and Fourré (1962) and Menzel (1962) produced conflicting results. In more recent studies the pattern has tended to emerge which is that absence rates are higher among day workers than shift-workers.

There are two ways of comparing the absences of shiftworkers. There is an internal comparison where the absence of the same men are compared when they work on the different shifts, eg day shift or night shift. Secondly, there is the comparison between separate groups of dayworkers and shiftworkers. Considering the first type of comparison Wyatt and Marriott (1953) recorded the absence rates of shiftworkers on alternate day/night shift for the weeks when they worked on days and the weeks when they worked on nights. In a group of workers who changed shifts every four weeks, absence rates were relatively low in the first week of the night shift and increased in subsequent weeks; on the day shift absence started at a relatively high level in the first week and declined in subsequent weeks. This is the same trend that occurs for output and reinforces the suggestion that fatigue accumulates on the night shift and is gradually dissipated on the subsequent day shift. Absence has been shown to differ over the shifts in other respects; Shepherd and Walker (1956) demonstrated that in a steel works 75 per cent of the single shift absence occurred on the morning shift of a three shift system. It is reported that the absence of miners is often high on the morning shift for they may be sent home or given a surface job if they attend for work after man winding is complete. This kind of absence may be related to fatigue, but it is also due to the early morning start and might be reduced by adjusting the starting and stopping times of the shifts. These internal comparisons are interesting but do not go far to answer the question of whether shiftworking affects health.

In considering the second type of comparison between separate groups of shiftworkers and dayworkers, one of the most exhaustive studies was made by Taylor and his associates (1972). They collected the absence figures of 965 pairs of men. One member of the pair was on daywork and the other on shiftwork. Each pair was matched for age and type of work and had to satisfy certain criteria of length of service and time of working on shifts. The study compared six types of shift system – three shift discontinuous, three shift continuous (traditional weekly rotation), three shift continuous (rapid rotation), permanent nights, alternate day/night and double days. It is important to note that any worker who was known to have transferred from shiftwork for medical reasons was excluded from the day work sample. Table 4.1 shows the overall results which demonstrate clearly that all types of absence – certified sickness, short sickness and other absence – were lower for shiftworkers than day workers.

As an example of the difference in percentage terms the day workers had 15 per cent more spells of sickness absences than the shiftworkers, 21 per cent more short sickness absences and 28 per cent more absences for other reasons. The next step was to compare the sickness absence of the shiftworkers and dayworkers according to the medical diagnosis. The certified sickness absences were classified into eight diagnostic groups, and there was a general trend in all except one of the groups for there to be a greater incidence of absence on the day shift, but none of the differences were statistically significant. The excess of absence on the day shift was not there due to any particular type of illness. It is notable that digestive disorders, bronchitis, mental and psycho-neurotic disorders and cardiovascular disorders, which have sometimes been associated with night work, were more often the cause of absence on day shiftwork. The one exception was peptic ulcers where there was a higher incidence among shiftworkers, but the difference was very slight; however, the authors conclude that on this evidence, the suggestion that shiftwork may be associated with this condition cannot be completely rejected. In general the trend of more absence on day work held when the

67

Table 4.1

Mean annual rates of absence in matched pairs of day and shiftworkers for 1968 and 1969

	Certified sickness		Short sickness		Other absence	
	Day	Shift	Day	Shift	Day	Shift
No of men	965	965	812	812	643	643
Spells/man year	0.77	0.67	1.70	1.41	0.68	0.53
Days/man year	12.13	9.54	2.53	2.11	0.93	0.71
Average length of spell	15.8	14.2	1.5	1.5	1.4	1.3

From Taylor P J, Pocock S J and Sergean R, Absenteeism of shift and Dayworkers, *British Journal of Industrial Medicine*, 29 208–213, 1972.

comparison was made with the six types of shift system. For certified sickness the trend was most marked for double day shift where sickness was about half the day shift rate, on the other hand there was slightly more sickness among the shiftworkers on the alternate day /night shift. The numbers in the different shiftworking groups tended to be small and the relationship between absence and different types of shiftwork awaits a further large scale study.

One recent study which has been widely quoted on the relation between absence, including sickness absence, and shiftwork is reported by the National Board for Prices and Incomes (1970). In this study all types of absence were slightly higher for shiftworkers than dayworkers. The study did attempt to control for age but there is no attempt to control for type of work and it is known that shiftworkers are more widely represented in the heavy end of industry, such as coal mining, iron and steel and metal manufacture. The result is therefore not surprising, and as a measure of the association between absence and shiftworking, is probably invalid. Nevertheless conflicting results still arise in the type of study described.

The reason why sickness and other absence among shiftworkers is generally found to be lower than among day workers is almost certainly due to selection. Shiftworkers who become ill may, on their own volition or on the advice of their doctor, transfer to day work. Other men who suffer ill health may never contemplate taking up shiftwork; shiftworkers are therefore a 'survivor population'. In most organizations, even if shiftwork is a condition of employment, men can move from shiftwork if they wish to do so as their length of service and seniority increases. There may be other reasons why absence is lower on shiftwork. Taylor (1967) interviewed a group of shiftworkers in an oil refinery; he found that they liked shiftwork, they had a high job satisfaction and they worked in smaller groups than the day workers which might have accounted for their lower absence rates. High morale among closely knit work groups is known to be a feature of shift crews and may be another reason why absence is lower among shiftworkers. Another attraction of shiftwork is the higher pay for the less popular shifts which acts as an incentive to attend. It has also been suggested that on the night shift there are fewer competing leisure attractions outside the factory, compared to the day shift when leisure opportunities are many and varied. It has been amply demonstrated (eg Taylor, 1968) that sickness absence is not only a response illness but is affected by conditions at work, social and domestic reasons and aspects of personality which may be unrelated to the illness. Selection is the most important reason why absence is lower among shiftworkers than dayworkers but there are also other reasons.

Selection may also operate in the other direction so that the less fit are attracted to shiftwork. Walker and de la Mare (1971) compared sickness and other absence of permanent nightworkers and dayworkers in three organizations. The nightworkers and dayworkers were matched for age and type of work. Absence in two of the groups was higher among the nightworkers. In both cases the pace of work was much lower at night, for instance in one group the units of output per man hour was about two thirds of the day shift. The results of interviewing a sample of the men suggested that the less hectic pace and generally more peaceful conditions on the night shift attracted some people who were less fit. In the third undertaking, a heavy engineering factory, the work load was exactly the same on the day and night shifts and the absence rates of the two shifts were about the same. It seemed in the two groups with higher absence on the night shift, that there was 'reverse' selection of less fit men onto the night shift. This kind of process could account for some of the inconsistencies in the results of studies relating sickness absence to shiftwork.

In conclusion most recent studies have shown more absence among day workers than shiftworkers: this is almost certainly due to selection of unfit shiftworkers onto day work, but other social and personal reasons may also be causes. The studies described, while they do not suggest that shiftwork can have a dramatic effect on health, do not answer the question definitively. Another approach is needed which is to carry out a longitudinal study of a group of shiftworkers and day workers over a period of years, recording their sickness absence and making clinical examinations. In this way account can be taken of those who transfer from shiftwork to day work. Aanonsen (1964) has carried out an excellent long term study.

A LONGITUDINAL STUDY

Aanonsen studied factory workers in three Norwegian electro-chemical works. The communities in which the men lived were relatively isolated and the work force was stable over the period of the study. The main purposes of the investigation were, firstly to study the effect on health of continuous shiftwork and to see if it gave rise to particular occupational diseases and secondly, to see if some people adapted more readily than others to shiftwork. The whole manual labour force were given annual medical examinations from 1948–53 when particular attention was paid to gastro-intestinal complaints, including peptic ulcer, nervous and cardiovascular disorders. In 1953 the examination included a range of physical measurements and an interview to obtain social information. For one calendar year detailed records of short and long sickness absences including medical diagnosis were recorded. There was also a retrospective study for the age group 55 – 65 years which extended over 13 years. The population of 1,106 manual workers was divided into three groups which were of approximately equal numbers. Workers who had been on shifts over the whole of the period, workers on days over the whole period and former shiftworkers who transferred to day work; this last group of ex-shiftworkers was further sub-divided into those who had changed onto day work for medical reasons and for other reasons.

The results of tabulating the absence rates and the medical consultations for the four groups are shown in table 4.2. It is seen that the dayworkers had slightly more spells of absence than the shiftworkers and considerably more (nearly 50 per cent) days of sickness absence. The former or ex-shiftworkers had more spells of absence than the dayworkers and about the same number of days lost through illness. It is therefore seen that the shiftworkers had the least absence with the dayworkers and ex-shiftworkers having about the same amount. Ex-shiftworkers who left for daywork because of medical reasons had more medical consultations than the other groups But whether a shiftworker changed to daywork for medical or other reasons did not seem to be related to sickness absence.

An exhaustive analysis was made of the symptoms and incidence of disorders in the three working goups which were thought to be affected by shiftwork: nervous, gastro-intestinal and cardiovascular. Cardiovascular disease was not associated with shiftwork. With nervous and gastro-intestinal conditions the incidence was much the same among shiftworkers and dayworkers, but much higher among ex-shiftworkers as table 4.3 shows.

Gastro-intestinal disorders including peptic ulcers were

Table 4.2

Absences and medical consultations among continuous shiftworkers, day workers and former shiftworkers who transferred to daywork for: (a) medical and (b) non-medical reasons in 1952

CATEGORY	Number	Spells of illness per worker		Worker per year	
		1–3 days	4 days or more	Days lost due to illness	Medical consultation
Continuous shiftworkers	373	0.58	0.34	6.25	3.39
Day workers	339	0.64	0.36	9.26	3.72
(a) Ex-shiftworkers who transferred for medical reasons	124	0.84	0.52	10.60	5.00
(b) Ex-shiftworkers who transferred for non-medical reasons	221	0.81	0.51	10.52	3.92

From Aanonsen A, *Shiftwork and Health*, 1964

Table 4.3
Percentage of day workers, shiftworkers, and former shiftworkers who transferred to day work for medical reasons suffering from nervous and gastro intestinal complaints

Diagnostic class	Dayworker	Shiftworker	Former shift-worker
Nervous disorders	13.3	10.5	32.8
Verified peptic ulcers	7.1 ⎤	6.1 ⎤	18.0 ⎤
Peptic symptoms without demonstrable ulcer	6.7 ⎬ 25.2	10.0 ⎬ 26.3	11.7 ⎬ 50.0
Other gastro-intestinal conditions	11.3 ⎦	10.2 ⎦	20.3 ⎦

From Aanonsen A, *Shiftwork and Health,* 1964

about twice as prevalent among the ex-shiftworkers, who had transferred to days for medical reasons, than among the dayworkers or shiftworkers; nervous disorders were nearly three times as prevalent among the ex-shift-workers. Aanonsen concluded:

> that former shift labourers comprised persons with a constitutional disposition to nervous and gastro-intestinal disorders in whom the stress of shiftwork in most instances precipitated the illness. Such labourers have special difficulties in adapting themselves to the ever changing sleeping hours and irregular meal times as well as to the restrictions imposed by shiftwork on spare time activities.

He goes on to add:

> the main reasons for the fact that the shiftworkers showed no greater morbidity than the dayworkers in

regard to nervous or gastro-intestinal disorders are that the former represented a highly selected material of permanent shiftworkers with a capacity of adaptation and fitness for this form of industrial work and that a continuous transfer had taken place of unsuitable labourers to other forms of work.

Finally, it is suggested that no disease is directly caused by shiftwork, but that people who have difficulty in adapting may develop nervous or gastro-intestinal disorders if they are susceptible to them.

GASTRO-INTESTINAL CONDITIONS

Numerous studies have been made on the effects of shiftwork on health and Menzel (1962) in his review of earlier studies examines those which test for an association between shiftwork and the three categories of disorders studied by Aanonsen – cardiovascular, nervous and gastro-intestinal. The last has sometimes shown a relationship with shiftwork; for instance in the 1940s and 1950s there were a series of studies in Scandinavia which on balance showed that there were more stomach disorders among shiftworkers than dayworkers and particularly there was a greater incidence of peptic ulcers. Description of the symptoms experienced by nightworkers included stomach pains and indigestion. However, the results of research are not consistent and Doll *et al* (1951) in Britain surveyed the incidence of peptic ulcer in a large population but failed to find any association between the disorder and shiftwork. They also found very few men who had transferred from shiftwork to daywork because of peptic ulcers.

Many of the studies were conducted 20 or more years ago when both diet and working conditions were of much lower standards than today. Further there has been a fall in the incidence of peptic ulcers in the population of

Western countries in the last 25 years. The causes have not been firmly established but the fall has averted an incidence of peptic ulcer which was reaching 'epidemic' proportions. It is also possible that as different occupational groups were studied the results may have been a function of occupation instead of shiftwork; for example, some of the early work was on railway staff and there are other reasons than irregular hours why the crews of steam locomotives might suffer peptic ulcers, such as dust and fumes, or variations in temperature. Another reason why shiftworkers may be predisposed to suffer gastritis is the unhygienic conditions in which they eat their meals in the factory and the unsuitable balance of their diet (see page 171). Rutenfranz *et al* (1976) wrote:

> because the social conditions for eating during the shifts are not good, because normal social family life is often interrupted by shiftwork, and shiftworkers tend towards irregular meals and types of food which are quick to prepare are preferred. Therefore shiftworkers' digestive disorders are often caused by irregular meals and an unbalanced diet. Short meal breaks under good social conditions and a balanced diet should therefore be offered as ergonomic measures.

In conclusion it seems that the evidence offered by Aanonsen is soundest, with the suggestion that although shiftwork does not cause illness, it may precipitate nervous and gastro-intestinal disorders in those who are susceptible to them. Then these men may leave shiftwork.

DISTURBANCE TO SLEEP

Disturbance to day-time sleep after a night shift is one of the commonest complaints. Aanonsen (1964) in the study previously described found that 89 per cent of former shiftworkers who transferred to day work for medical reasons had experienced difficulties in sleeping but following the transfer to day work only 16 per cent complained of sleeping badly. In another Scandinavian study Thiis-Evansen (1958) found that 60 per cent of shiftworkers as compared to 11 per cent of day workers suffered from sleep disturbance and he pointed out that fatigue seemed to build up over the sequence of night shifts and it did not disperse until the succeeding day shift. The nervous disorders to which shiftworkers are susceptible and tend to suffer from have been attributed to the difficulty of obtaining sleep during the day. Wyatt and Marriott (1953) found that only 58 per cent of the workers they interviewed were satisfied with the amount and quality of their sleep and the remainder were not; even among those who were satisfied many said that the day-time sleep was less refreshing than sleep at the normal time. These high proportions of shiftworkers reporting sleep disturbances are not always found, for instance Taylor (1967) showed that only 16 per cent of the shiftworkers he interviewed complained of difficulty in sleeping, nearly always following a night shift. Nevertheless, the balance of evidence suggests that some people never manage to adapt their sleeping habits during the day and as a result leave shiftwork: it seems to be this lack of adjustment of sleeping habits which compel men to leave. Others who manage to continue shiftwork still have difficulty in sleeping, but the exact proportion of men varies and will depend on the type of shift, the degree of selection to the shiftworking group and the home conditions for sleeping during the day. Disturbance to sleep may affect both its quantity and quality.

Table 4.4 shows the hours of sleep of 109 continuous shiftworkers drawn from a chemical and iron and steel works on rapidly rotating shift systems (Walker, 1966). The table shows the amount of continuous sleep before the morning shift and after the night and afternoon shifts.

Table 4.4
Men on rapidly rotating continuous shift systems. Hours of continuous sleep before the morning shift and after the afternoon and night shifts

Shift	Continuous hours of sleep								Number of men
	3– <4	4– <5	5– <6	6– <7	7– <8	8– <9	9– <10	>10	
am*	—	8	58	35	7	1	—	—	109
pm	—	—	—	1	6	20	42	34	103
night*	8	21	26	22	16	10	2	1	106

*Frequently supplemented by rest later in the day

From Walker J, Frequent alternation of shifts on continuous work, *Occupational Psychology*, 40, 215–225, 1966.

The shift hours were 06.00 – 14.00, 14.00 – 22.00 and 22.00 – 06.00. The results show that the amount of continuous sleep was least before the morning shift and after the night shift. But in both cases the long period of sleep was often supplemented by naps or dozing off in a chair later in the day. It was not possible to combine the continuous sleep with the additional rest because the men themselves were unaware of the duration of their second period of sleep. Sleeping habits were fairly uniform among the men before the morning shift and after the afternoon shift, but very variable after the night shift. Nearly all the men went to bed within an hour or so of arriving home from the night shift, some then slept throughout the day and got up in time for the evening meal with the rest of the family. Others slept a few hours in the morning, got up for the midday meal and either rested or went back to bed later in the day. The amount and regularity of sleep was least satisfactory after the night shift, next sleep was curtailed by the early morning start before the morning shift, but after the afternoon shift and on their days off the men took the opportunity to lie in and compensate for any 'sleep debt' which had accumulated during the more arduous shifts.

Of 315 shiftworkers surveyed by Wedderburn (1975a), 47 per cent found the irregular sleep disturbing and this was correlated with a dislike of shiftwork. He points out that the recovery which is possible through sleeping longer on the afternoon shift and days off is an argument for rapidly rotating shifts where, unlike six or seven shifts in succession, there is no danger of building up a 'sleep debt'. 'Our studies convince me' writes Wedderburn 'that adequate quantities of sleep are both more important and more obtainable than adaptation of circadian rhythms to working at night'. He goes on to add that the shortage of sleep which most workers experience as a result of their abnormal hours comes well within the normal range of sleep of active people who display wide individual differences in the amount of sleep they normally need.

A picture of sleep patterns of shiftworkers very similar to that described above, was found by Tune (1969) who asked a group of 52 qualified engineers on three shiftwork to keep a diary recording their hours of sleep and wakefulness. Diary keeping provides a more accurate record of sleeping hours than asking shiftworkers questions in an interview. The 52 engineers were matched with 52 day workers and it was found that the shiftworkers slept somewhat longer than the non-shiftworkers (16 minutes on average) and they took longer and more frequent naps outside their main sleep period. However the diaries demonstrated that when they were working their sleep was shorter and was more broken into episodes, ie of naps and snoozes than normal sleep and they built up a 'sleep debt'. This was 'paid off' or even 'over compensated' during their non working days. Tune suggests that the most important aspect may be the quality of the shiftworkers' sleep.

Many men do complain of the quality of their sleep during the day. They say it is disturbed by daytime noise which may come from either outside or inside the house. Traffic noise and the noise from tradesmen disturb shiftworkers' sleep; in this connection the sound of the bells from ice-cream vans on the roads of housing estates come in for particularly acid comments from shift-workers. Noise from children is also disturbing and the shiftworkers' wives have to learn to do their housework quietly or postpone it until after their husbands have awakened from their day-time sleep. Aanonsen (1964) found that poor housing conditions were the commonest cause of sleep difficulties. Nearly three-quarters of the shiftworkers who were in poor housing suffered sleep difficulties, often pronounced, while only 18 per cent of the day shift workers with poor housing slept badly. Accommodation which is suitable for a dayworker may be unsuitable for a shiftworker who requires a bedroom where he can sleep undisturbed during the day. Similarly accommodation which may be good for a married couple can become unsuitable when the shiftworker's wife has a child. In Norway the housing difficulties of shiftworkers have been taken seriously and at least one organization has attempted to better their housing by attending to the site of the house, its insulation and the location of a bedroom.

Some objective evidence of the disturbance to the quality of daytime sleep is becoming available. This is provided by recording the electrical activity of the brain continuously during daytime sleep, after a night shift. The records can then be compared with those obtained during normal sleep at night. The results from these studies are equivocal. There seems to be some changes in
80

the phasing of the different levels of sleep particularly deep sleep and some changes in the spells of rapid eye movement (REM) sleep, both of which are thought to be related to the quality of sleep. Some experiments have also shown a shortening in the length of day time compared to night-time sleep. Using the same methods imaginative experiments have been conducted on the effects of noise on daytime sleep. In one of these (Knauth and Rutenfranz, 1975) the experimental subjects were submitted to either traffic noise or children's noise. Both disturbed the daytime sleep as measured by electrical activity in the brain and rapid eye movements but the children's noise disturbed sleep more than the traffic noise, although it was less intense, probably because the children's noise varied more. The experimenters concluded that a shortening of the length and a deterioration in the quality of nightworkers' day-time sleep must be expected. This work has a long way to go before it produces results which have practical value. But in time it may be able to answer such questions as whether it is better for a nightworker to rest before he goes on the night shift, or whether it is better to keep awake so that he thoroughly tires himself out and sleeps soundly after the shift the next day.

Given that the experience of shiftworkers and experimental evidence both show that shiftworkers often have their sleep reduced in quality and quantity after a night shift what effect does this have on their behaviour? As has been noted some shiftworkers transfer to daywork for this reason; some complain of tiredness and irritability on the night shift which extends into the home situation. Mott *et al* (1965) asked the shiftworkers in their survey whether the loss of sleep due to their work schedule affected:

how well you get along with your wife
being the kind of husband you want to be
getting along with your children
being the kind of father you want to be
going out socially.

The results are as follows:–

	A big effect	Some effect
going out socially	26%	30%
how well you get along with your wife	12%	34%
being the kind of husband you want to be	14%	34%
getting along with your children	10%	32%
being the kind of father you want to be	13%	32%

The results show that more than a quarter of the 714 shiftworkers found that the effects of loss of sleep had a big effect on their social life. Substantial minorities also found that the effects of lack of sleep affected their roles as husband and father. Whether the shiftworkers can distinguish between the effects of loss of sleep and the effects of other disturbances to the body is, of course, a moot point.

In the factory situation it is almost impossible to show if lack of sleep affects output – for one reason sleep loss is inextricably mixed up with the disturbance to other circadian rhythms. In the laboratory it has been shown that performance on tasks, similar to those described in the last chapter in connection with the effects of bodily rhythms, shows a drop after quite small deficits in the amount of sleep. The tasks have to be simple, sedentary and boring to the subjects. That is the kind of tasks which induce drowsiness or low arousal. If however the tasks are stimulating and are enjoyed by the subjects then long periods of sleep deprivation have no effect on performance (Wilkinson, 1964). Naval ratings were able to complete complex interesting tasks like playing a game of battleships after more than 40 hours sleep deprivation, but they were quite unable to complete tasks which they found uninteresting. Tasks which demand continuous attention are also more likely to be affected by loss of sleep than those which are intermittent. Combating the effects of loss of sleep on performance and taking remedial action involve similar steps to those outlined on page 55 in connection with the effects of circadian rhythms. Sleep deprivation of 24 hours occurs among shiftworkers where the practice is adopted of asking a man to work a double shift as a relief for someone who is absent. This is not uncommon and means a stretch of 16 hours work.

SUBJECTIVE FEELINGS OF MALAISE

The evidence surveyed has not proven that shiftwork causes ill health and perhaps the most satisfactory way of describing adverse physical affects of shiftwork is that they induce feelings of malaise. All the studies which have used interviews as a method of obtaining information from shiftworkers elicited complaints of the effects of nightwork on physical well being. The complaints relate to habits associated with the diurnal cycle – sleeping, eating and elimination. Complaints are therefore of sleeplessness and fatigue, headache, stomach pains, indigestion, dyspepsia, constipation, loss of appetite, 'nerves', depression and allied disturbances. Menzel (1962) quotes from a number of studies in a wide range of industries, from iron and steel to textiles, where the workers made these kind of complaints; their prevalence was high in the study of Wyatt and Marriott (1953) among alternate day and night shiftworkers, which is a particularly demanding system, because of the amount of nightwork. More recently a survey (Mott *et al*, 1965) found that three per cent of day workers, six per cent of workers on fixed afternoon shifts, eight per cent of permanent night workers and 14 per cent of rotating shiftworkers were greatly affected by disturbances to their 'time oriented body functions' and in addition about half of the men interviewed made some complaints.

Although account must be taken of the complaints by a large number of shiftworkers of minor ailments, it is not necessary to accept them all as being a consequence of shiftwork. Dirken (1966) asked about 600 Dutch shiftworkers and 1200 non-shiftworkers to complete a health questionnaire. The respondents were not told that shiftworking was being investigated, unlike nearly all other surveys. The results showed that there were *not* more complaints among shiftworkers; in particular gastro-intestinal and nervous complaints were *not* associated with shiftwork. There was a slightly lower feeling of general well-being among the shiftworkers, although this was not of an extent to be considered a problem. Shiftworkers were also more liable than day workers to fall asleep at home in a chair. The author explained the failure of an association between complaints about health and shiftwork to the men being highly selected, in that those who had not adjusted had moved to other work.

PREVENTIVE ACTION

General preventive measures to minimize the effects of shiftwork on health can take two forms, either to attend to the individual shiftworker or to pay attention to the conditions under which the shiftwork is organized. The preventive measures for individual shiftworkers include:

84

pre-employment medical examinations and the selection of shiftworkers (see page 155)

allowing those who experience ill health, sleeplessness, etc to transfer to day work

providing advice on the hygiene of shiftwork, eg personal habits, diet.

The steps that can be taken to provide a suitable organization of shiftwork include:

ensure that excessive hours are not worked either through overtime or working too long hours at a stretch

see that the shift rotas allow frequent breaks for rest and leisure, particularly that adequate off-duty time follows the night shift

attend to ergonomic and hygiene factors in the working situation, eg design of work, environmental conditions, adequate breaks, etc. This is even more important on shifts than on days

ensure that the shiftworker is provided with adequate facilities during the night, eg hygienic eating arrangements, first aid or nursing attendance.

CHAPTER 5

҈҉҈҉҈҉҈҉҈҉҈

Effects on social and family life

There are some useful ideas for thinking about the effects of shiftwork on social and family life, which have been formulated by social scientists. One of these is the notion of 'marginality'. It is commonplace to talk of shiftworking as abnormal, nightwork as unnatural, shiftworkers as being isolated and so forth. These sayings all imply that the shiftworker is in an unnatural relationship to the other members of his community and in a sense apart from them. He may be thought of as a 'marginal man', that is to say he is functioning in his work and in social life on the margins of his community so that he may not be accepted by or interact effectively with other members of it. To make the analogy clear another example of 'marginal man' are the practitioners who are on the fringes of medicine such as the osteopaths who act as healers but are not accepted by the medical profession and do not enjoy recognition in the health service system, nor in many cases from the community in which they work. They can therefore be said to function in their occupations on the margins of the healing professions. It might be possible to order shiftworkers into the effectiveness with which they are able to play a full part in the community according to the hours they work. Thus on multiple shifts the double day shift might be the least handicapped and the permanent nightwork the most with rotating three shifts in between. There are two concepts which are useful in exploring the difficulties of shiftworkers. The first is role: how effectively can the shiftworker fulfil the roles he is expected to play in the community? The second is the 'social dimension' of time: how does the shiftworker cope with disorganization to the normal temporal patterns of his social and domestic life?

Every member of society fills a number of roles and most waking activities are concerned with filling a role in relation to other individuals or groups. A person's family roles are perhaps the most important to him and the shiftworker has among other family roles those of husband and father. He has to engage in certain activities such as supplying companionship, emotional support and satisfying the sexual needs of his wife; he has to provide companionship to his children, to act as a model for them and to participate in aspects of their rearing and education. Similarly the shiftworker is expected in his family role to be the breadwinner and to provide for the family. At work in the factory his role will largely be determined by his job, eg fitter, turner, machinist, or foreman, but it will also be partly determined by his being a shiftworker. Outside work and the family settings most people fill various social roles, either in relation to institutional organizations such as the church, a political party, a sporting club, or in the more informal spontaneous activities of visiting friends or drinking with workmates. The shiftworker may follow solitary activities such as reading or fishing which involve no apparent social role, although they may help in social activities as he can talk about his reading or the size of the fish he has caught. Mott *et al* (1965) have usefully defined the ways in which shiftwork can interfere with the performance of a person's normal roles.

Shiftwork can prevent the carrying out of role function,

in that the shiftworker may be deprived of participating in activities which take place when he is working or resting but when most members of the community are enjoying their leisure, eg by watching or taking part in sport. On the other hand the shiftworker may find it easier to fill certain roles, for instance in family life by helping his wife with the shopping during the day or taking his children on outings during their school holidays. Some advantages of shiftworking are very often overlooked by the non-shiftworker including the social scientist, but they can be real compensations to the shiftworker. Shiftwork can also interfere with activities of other members of the family. A shiftworker's wife may have to postpone her housework while her husband is resting, or prepare extra meals for him, and the children may have to curtail their play while their father is sleeping during the day. Because the shiftworker is working 'unsocial' hours his whereabouts is unpredictable to other people so that his friends and relations do not include him when they plan their recreation and he becomes isolated. Finally, although shiftwork does not alter the amount of time the shiftworker has available, it may alter qualitatively the way he fills his roles, for instance, he may belong to a society or a club but be unable to become an office holder because of his irregular attendance.

All these effects can and do occur but their prevalence and the degree to which they qualitatively change shiftworkers' lives has to be investigated.

The second concept which is useful in thinking about the domestic and social life of shiftworkers is 'social time'. Just as physical activities follow a diurnal pattern, so too do social and domestic activities when, for example, social and family activities are pursued in the evening, work during the day, with certain times for meals and attending to personal needs. Superimposed on the diurnal cycle of activities is the weekly cycle with extended time for leisure at the weekend. It is clear that the community's activities are geared to the dayworker's cycle of work and rest and only incidentally take account of the shiftworkers whose lives depart from the normal pattern. The analogy which has sometimes been used is an economic one (Blakelock, 1960; Bullock *et al*, 1974) rather than a biological comparison. Time is said to have different liquidity and exchange value according to the time of the day and the day of the week. Evenings have a high value to workers with the highest point at the weekends. The exchange value of a Saturday evening is very high for single people. In parts of one large British industry in the public sector the informal practice has evolved of a worker who wants free time paying a fellow worker to take over an unpopular shift. Some shifts command no premium but others at the weekend or on a Bank Holiday command a high exchange rate which the shiftworker has to pay to get an off duty colleague to work his shift for him. Variations in the shiftwork premia are a further recognition of the value of certain times to the shiftworker. Conversely some parts of the day are not highly valued by many people such as free time in the morning when some shiftworkers complain it is wasted time and they may occupy it by sleeping longer than their physiological needs demand. One group of research workers at Cambridge (Bullock *et al*, 1974) have written about time budgets and have asked people to keep diaries of the time and location of their activities over the 24 hours. It is possible to build up accurate pictures of how a community distributes its time over different activities and in which locations. The diary keepers can be sub-divided by age, sex, etc to arrive at a detailed descriptive account of community activities. The resulting information is potentially useful for planning purposes.

Shiftworkers will have quite different time budgets from normal day workers, but there have not been, as yet, any extensive studies. Small scale diary keeping experiments of shiftworkers have been attempted (eg Caillot, 1959; de la Mare and Walker, 1968) but it would be useful if the techniques of Bullock and his associates were applied extensively to shiftworkers on different systems.

Another aspect of 'social time' is the flexibility of different activities (Blakelock, 1960; Vroom, 1964). Some activities are completely flexible and can be carried out at any time during daylight hours and they include gardening or walking. Then there are activities with limited flexibility such as the time of family meals, which can be adjusted within narrow limits, or the shiftworker can adjust his times of eating by, for example, delaying his main meal after a night shift till the evening when he can eat with other members of the family. Finally there are activities which are highly specific to a particular time such as watching a sporting event or a TV programme. The activities which a shiftworker can engage in when off duty will depend mainly on which shift he is working and the degree with which his interests are dependent on other people or institutionalized arrangements. If the shiftworker is able to develop interests which are temporally flexible he is more likely to enjoy his free time than if he clings to activities which can only be carried out at specific times.

EFFECTS ON DOMESTIC LIFE

The effects of shiftwork on domestic life are mixed and it is difficult to quantify them, partly because the number of studies are limited and the results are conflicting. There is no doubt that shiftwork and particularly nightwork can have a disruptive effect on the shiftworker's family life and the irregular hours of the husband puts an extra burden on the shiftworker's wife. The effects can be divided, in theory, into those which disorganize the running of the household and the effects on personal relationships among the family members, but in practice the one is closely related to the other as, for instance, the wife preparing meals for the husband at awkward times which can cause irritation between them.

Brown (1959) has itemized the effects of nightwork which shiftworkers' wives dislike. They are:

interference with the daily work in the home because the husband is asleep or in the way
wife nervous when alone at night
wife lonely in the evening
strain of keeping children quiet
wife cannot go out in the evening
problem of feeding the husband
irritable husband.

It is seen that the wife's dislikes centre round the husband being at home at the 'wrong' times. He is in the way during the day particularly when the wife wants to get on with her housework and the children need to play. There is the problem of feeding a husband after a nightshift which has been graphically described by Brown:

For many men (on the night shift) there was no time of day or night when they really wanted a hot dinner. The time when this was normally provided was about 5.00 pm or 6.00 pm but, as one woman said, she did not know when her husband would get up in the evening for his evening meal or whether he would want it when he got up. Many men did not feel that they wanted a heavy meal when they had just got out of bed, nor did they want it just before they were going to work. One woman said that every meal she gave her husband was like a breakfast.

Maurice (1975) quotes continental studies which show clearly that the difficulties of the housewife are worse if housing standards are poor or she has a large family. One study showed that resting during the day was difficult for 55 per cent of shiftworkers where the family had two rooms, in 41 per cent of cases where the family had three rooms, in 27 per cent of cases where it had four rooms, and in only 8 per cent of cases where it had five rooms. The shiftworker may be at home at inconvenient times but he is also away from home at the 'wrong' times. Many wives dislike being left at home on their own in the evening and at night when their husbands are at work. They find the evenings lonely and feel nervous and anxious at night in their husband's absence. It was found by de la Mare and Walker (1968) that one of the most important reasons that a group of telegraphists on day shift declined to work nights was their wives' dislike of being left alone in the house.

There are compensating advantages to wives of having their husbands at home during the day. These include:

he helps at home when she is at work
he helps with the children
he helps at home (eg on Mondays)
he helps with the shopping
more leisure together
enjoyment of outings together.

To the working wife having her husband at home during the day can have real advantages if he is prepared to help with the domestic work. On the other hand with both working on different shift systems there are long periods when they scarcely see each other. When the wife is not at work she often sees more of him than if he was on day work, particularly day work with overtime. If he can adapt to night work by sleeping soundly during the day and enjoys his meals there can be little disturbance to his wife's routine. He may also help her about the house, assist her in shopping and take an active interest in 'do it yourself' improvements. He sees more of his children under school age and more of the older children during the school holidays. He can take them on outings and motor during the week when the roads to the coast and country are relatively uncrowded. They can enjoy the higher standard of living which his extra earnings bring. If the husband cannot adapt physically and suffers from lack of sleep, indigestion or irritability then the family will not be able to enjoy these potential advantages of shiftwork.

The effects of shiftwork have been looked at in a rather different way by Mott *et al* (1965) who examined the roles of husband and wife and their personal relationships. They asked shiftworkers and their wives if they thought it was easier or harder to take part in the main activities of family life on shiftwork or on day work. Questions were asked about the following aspects of the marriage – companionship – assistance with housework – providing diversion and relaxation – protection of wife from harm – mutual understanding – decision making – sexual relationships. On the whole the shiftworkers found it less easy to provide for these activities adequately in their marriages than if they had worked on day shift. But their replies differed according to whether they wished to change to daywork or not, as those who wished to move off shiftwork were less well adjusted in their family life than those who wished to remain on shifts. Shiftworkers also had difficulty in fulfilling their roles as fathers, but being a shiftworker's wife did not seem to affect the mother's role. The investigators then went on to study the effects of shiftwork on marital happiness and family integration and they concluded that there was a two stage effect upon marriage and family. First of all the conflict between the hours at work and the times usually given over to family activities resulted in difficulty and interference in family life. Secondly there seems to be a cumulative effect of these various interferences with role performance leading to some reduction in marital happiness and an even greater reduction in the ability to co-ordinate family activities and to minimize strain and friction among family members. These results rely on opinions of shiftworkers and must be accepted with caution. Research workers have looked for evidence of shiftwork breaking up marriages but it has not been forthcoming. Even when a marriage of a shiftworker is in difficulty he may have chosen to work shifts to escape from his marital problems. There is one piece of positive evidence in that the National Child Development Study in England which has followed the progress of 16,000 children since their birth in 1958 shows that whatever effects shiftwork may have on the family it does not impair school performance or emotional adjustment of the shiftworker's children (Lambert and Hart, 1976).

An interesting example of shiftworker's wives disliking the interference to their normal domestic and social routine is supplied by Banks (1956, 1960). She interviewed the wives of steelworkers who had changed from a three shift discontinuous system with free weekends to a three shift continuous system with days off on varying days of the week. The wives did not complain about changes in the domestic routine but they were disappointed and even embittered at being deprived of their social life with their husbands at weekends. His free week days when he was at home did not compensate for the lost weekends. This might be understandable when the wife works and was, herself, only free at the weekend but the feeling went beyond this and women who did not work and without children still felt that the weekend was the 'proper' time to go out and enjoy leisure. The husbands shared the view of their wives and made such comments as 'we like to go out at the weekend. If you are at home on washing day you can't do much, can you?' or 'more time at home but no enjoyment in it'.

Too little is known about the effects of shiftwork on domestic life and it is difficult to make generalizations. Adjustment of domestic life to the demands of irregular hours depends on the ability of the individual family to restructure its way of living. If this is achieved then some of the advantages of shiftwork can be exploited and disturbance to family life may be slight; where the family is unable to make the adjustment it will lead to dissatisfaction.

EFFECTS ON SOCIAL LIFE

A number of studies* have been carried out on the social effects of shiftwork, often in conjunction with a change in industrial technology, eg to more automated plant. The extent to which unusual hours affect the social life of the shift worker is difficult to determine and varies according to local circumstances such as the nature of the shift system or the locality of the works or the length of time the men have worked shifts. Nevertheless the general pattern of what happens to the social life of shiftworkers is becoming clear. It may be divided into:

*See, for example, studies of printers (Lipset, Trow and Coleman, 1956), oil refinery workers (Blakelock, 1960), power station workers (Mann and Hoffman, 1960), Steel Workers (Banks, 1960; Chadwick-Jones, 1969) and railwaymen (Salaman, 1974). There are two more general studies (Brown, 1959; Mott *et al* 1965) and descriptive accounts of the social and sociological implications of shiftwork (Brown, 1975; Maurice, 1975).

organizational membership and institutional activities
contacts with friends and relatives
solitary or near solitary activities.

The results of the studies generally confirm expectations arising from shiftworkers' unusual hours and the distribution of 'social time' in the community. Membership of organizations may not always be lower among shiftworkers, except perhaps for joining sports clubs, but the shiftworker finds it much more difficult to take part in the activities of organizations to which he does belong and it may be impossible for a shiftworker to become a member of a committee or an office holder. He may also find it difficult to attend evening classes in adult education. These findings are, of course, expected but they are important, for participation in a community's voluntary organizations has been taken as a sign of social integration and the vitality of a society. It is the cause of some concern if a large minority of workers are partially excluded from taking an active part in institutional life.

The findings regarding the shiftworkers' interaction with friends and relatives are more equivocal. There is some indication that shiftworkers find it more difficult to make friends, for they cannot be relied on to provide companionship at set times; they also find it difficult to come to set family occasions such as anniversaries. But as regards social visiting to friends and neighbours or seeing relations in the extended family, shiftworkers seem able to manage this as easily and as frequently as day workers. These meetings are informal and often spontaneous, even when they are arranged their timing is flexible. Shiftworkers have been found to associate with other shiftworkers and in the north of England there are working men's social clubs the opening hours of which cater for shiftworkers' needs. Visiting friends and relatives does not appear to be a major problem for shiftworkers.

We have noted that the shiftworker is at an advantage in carrying out day-time and outside activities. One study found that just as many dayworkers as shiftworkers garden, fish or carry out home improvements but the shiftworker has much greater opportunity to pursue these hobbies. They have often been referred to as solitary pursuits and they can be carried out without relying on other people, but Sergean (1971) has pointed out that the allotment can be the hub of an active social network and an angling club can be very social. In a large city the shiftworker can find organized recreation and entertainment during the day with other people but in rural or small urban areas most recreational activity is centred round the weekend when the shiftworker may be working.

The social activities of shiftworkers and the difficulties he experiences are fairly predictable but whether they are viewed by the shiftworker as a hardship depends on:

the shiftworker's personal characteristics
the rota he is on
the kind of community he lives in.

There is evidence (page 157) that young single people, married men without children and the older person are under-represented in the population of shiftworkers, while married men in the middle years of their working life are over-represented among shiftworkers. Shiftworking is unpopular among young, single men as it interferes too much with their active social life and dating so that they avoid hours which mean working in the evening or at the weekend. The older worker may find the stress of working shifts too much. However the married man with domestic responsibilities finds the money an incentive to work shifts. He may have mortages to pay off

97

and a growing family to support. The shiftwork allowances enable the worker to maintain a higher standard of living, for instance to run a car or have a family holiday. At all times when a family is expanding and the children are growing up there are desirable material goals which the family wishes to achieve so that the shiftworker, when he has reached one material goal, has another to aim for.

There is evidence that in shiftworking communities, eg mining villages, the shiftworker is accepted and is accorded high status but when shiftworkers are not a numerous group both they and their neighbours consider that they are on jobs of lower social status. As Brown (1975) writes, shiftwork 'even if it does provide the opportunity for a middle class consumption pattern, it denies the worker some of the social prestige normally associated with such consumption'. The low prestige of shiftwork may be another reason why people without heavy financial commitments avoid it. There may be other characteristics of people such as personality which make shifts socially unacceptable but they have not as yet been adequately investigated.

Shift systems have different effects on social life according to the arrangements of the rotas. Some social consequences of double day shift and rapidly rotating shifts are discussed in chapter 6. Each shift also has its own social effects. On three shift working the morning shift is generally the most popular as the working and leisure hours correspond most closely to normal living. The early start on the shift means that the shiftworker should retire early the night before if he is to arrive at work fresh in the morning. This interferes with normal family and social life, although in practice many shiftworkers build up a sleep 'debt'. The afternoon shift is the least popular one socially and is much disliked by young single people who are prevented from enjoying their normal social interests.

If fixed shifts are worked the afternoon shift is more difficult to man. However some older men prefer the afternoon shift because of the opportunity for rest. The night shift is sometimes preferred to the afternoon shift because it provides some opportunity for normal social life up to 20.00 or 21.00 hours in the evening. One advantage of rapidly rotating shifts is that it helps to overcome the social deprivations of shiftwork. If the rotation is at longer intervals than a week then the worker spends a long spell on the afternoon shift which is either succeeded or preceded by the night shift: during both periods he finds himself 'socially dead'.

Shift systems also vary in their acceptability for social reasons as has been discussed elsewhere. The double day shift, although it has the advantage of no night working, makes social life difficult, for half the shiftworker's time at work is spent on the afternoon shift. The weekend is free, as it is on the discontinuous three shift system. Continuous three shiftwork is probably the system with the most disadvantages socially for in addition to the afternoon and night shifts the worker can only enjoy one weekend free in four.

A third factor which affects the social acceptability of shiftwork is the type of community the shiftworker lives in. Sociologists have described 'occupational communities' where the worker has a special relationship between his working life and his non-work life. He carries his working life into his leisure time so that the one is almost an extension of the other. His friends are his workmates and their conversation and chat is largely about work matters. He identifies himself with his job which is skilled and sometimes dangerous and he takes a great interest in it. Members of an occupational community live apart from other members of society and consider themselves to be separate. Sometimes they live in one locality but this does not seem to be a necessary condition to establish an occupational community. Sometimes its members are bound by rules and regulations which are imposed on them during their off duty hours, eg policemen. These are some of the characteristics of an occupational community. Descriptive accounts have been given of printers, fishermen, steelworkers, miners, policemen, jazz musicians and railwaymen.

Salaman (1974) made a study of a closely integrated group of railwaymen in Cambridge who formed an occupational community. They interacted socially, mainly with each other, and 47 per cent of them said they had four or more workmates as friends. The investigator points out that:

> the railwaymen in the sample were friendly with their workmates, rather than with other members of their occupation, because the times they worked made it difficult to get to know people except when they were at work.

Nearly all the railwaymen said that their out of work life was affected by the irregular hours of work, often adversely. It was one of the conditions which bound them together as a group even forcing them to mix together. it is notable that all the occupations listed above either work shifts or irregular hours and this is one of the conditions which leads to the formation of an occupational community although shiftwork is not, of itself, sufficient to do so.

The traditional occupational communities are breaking up. Chadwick-Jones (1969) has studied the break up of occupational communities which formerly were centred around the small tinplate hand-rolling mills in South Wales. The mills were situated in the same villages or townships in which the workers lived. They walked to and from work together and the work itself was arduous and not without danger. They were on a discontinuous three shift system. The small works were then abandoned for a large automated plant set at some distance from where the workers lived. They changed to a three shift continuous system. The occupational community tended to disintegrate as it was impossible to maintain old social habits. The men regretted the passing of the old ways, but it is not so certain that their wives did for they were pleased to see their husbands at home during their days off during the week. Small works and mines are being rationalized into large ones, people live further away from work which has tended to become less physical and safer so that the features which bound people together into an integrated community, to the exclusion of outsiders, are weakening. Occupational communities are disappearing but where they still exist shiftworking is often one of their features.

DOUBLE JOBBING

Double jobbing, or moonlighting as it is known in America, is frequently associated with shiftwork. This is the practice of holding a second job, usually a subsidiary one, in addition to one's main job. Many managers are none too keen on double jobbing because it may have an adverse affect on a man's factory job. It may cause fatigue so that the worker is incapable of performing his job effectively, or it may lead to a transfer of interest to the outside activity, leading to a weakening of motivation at work. Other workers intrigued and perhaps somewhat envious of the double jobber exaggerate the amount of extra money he earns. It is difficult to obtain objective evidence of the amount of double jobbing by shiftworkers which creates an uncertain situation conducive to the growth of rumour. In America Mott et al (1965) found that 11 per cent of workers on days, 19 per cent on afternoon shifts, 23 per cent on night shifts and 10 per cent on rotating shifts had second jobs. Thus the two fixed shifts, permanent afternoons and permanent nights which allowed for free time during the day, lead to more double jobbing. The rotating shiftworkers were no more likely to have second jobs than the day workers. A study in France (Maurice and Monteil, cited by Maurice, 1975) produced contradictory results. They found that 12 per cent of permanent shift, 14 per cent of rotating two shift, 27 per cent of discontinuous three shift and 33 per cent of continuous shiftworkers held second jobs. So that it was the three shift rotating workers who were most likely to have a double job. In Britain 3.3 per cent of all male employed workers hold a second job (Alden, 1976 a,b) but this is no indication of the proportion of shiftworkers double jobbing. Alden found that 20 per cent of second jobs held in a Cardiff study, were entirely week day jobs and many of these may have been held by shiftworkers. He also quotes an American study which showed that workers on a four day week were about twice as likely to hold a second job than those on a full week.

The figures on double jobbing are confusing and a more useful way of looking at the practice is to consider the type of work and the hours of second jobs. Many second jobs are a remunerative hobby or a profitable sideline. Alden found that most second jobs were service work held for only a small number of hours each week, typically about ten hours, and a third of the jobs were held in a self employed capacity. Gardening and small holding, window cleaning, home repairs and decorating, taxi-driver or part time barman are the kind of jobs carried out. Other work is seasonal, such as helping with fruit picking or part time jobs during the tourist season in certain areas. The people involved in double jobbing are
102

certainly amongst the most energetic in the community as nearly a third of them also work an average of eight hours overtime in their main job.

The objections of managers, which have been mentioned, are that double jobbing will affect performance on a man's main job and they are usually able to point to one or two specific cases of workers holding down two full time jobs. It is also possible that double jobbing can cause absenteeism. A variant of this theme has been put forward by Downie (1963) that double jobbers often drive, perhaps as taxi or coach drivers. The law limits the amount of time that commercial vehicle drivers can work but there is nothing stopping a man completing a night shift and then taking a vehicle out for a day's driving. Other criticisms from a different point of view are that double jobbing undermines the progress to shorter hours, or that in times of unemployment it deprives people of jobs. It is difficult to obtain evidence on these points and the tendency is to generalize too widely from particular instances. Many part time occupations are in the nature of a rewarding hobby and can be relaxing after a shift and due rest. Some are carried out in the open air and can be healthy and refreshing and the fact that the job is remunerative may be the only feature to distinguish it from energetic 'do it yourself' activities or gardening.

To conclude this section on social life, there is no doubt that shiftwork can and does interfere with it; but there are compensating advantages and the shiftworker has to balance the advantages and disadvantages in social and recreational activities. Whether the shiftworker finds the balance favourable or not depends on his own recreational interests and those of his family: it depends on his age and marital status, for specific interests are associated with different ages and stages of family development and

103

it depends also on the length of time he has worked on shifts and how well he adjusts to them physically.

ATTITUDES TO SHIFTWORK

The effects of shiftwork on the individual have been thoroughly explored in the last three chapters: the effects on circadian rhythms and performance; on health and sleep; on social and family life have been examined and it seems appropriate to conclude this section by asking what is the worker's overall attitude to shiftwork? If he weighs up the pros and cons in the balance what is the result? It must be acknowledged that the answers to the questions are by no means clear.

Table 5.1 shows the replies in two surveys to a question asking shiftworkers their overall attitude to working shifts.

The first is an American survey (Mann and Hoffman, 1960) in two power plants where the men were on continuous shiftwork. The second is a Dutch survey of a representative cross section of shiftworkers in a variety of factories (Drenth *et al*, 1976). A third survey shown is that carried out by the National Board for Prices and Incomes (1971) with a cross section of workers very similar to those selected in the Dutch study. It is also possible to show in the British study the results for continuous three shift workers who are comparable to those in the American survey. The question asked in the British survey was rather different and related to satisfaction with the shift system worked.

The results of the three surveys are quite different. In comparing the two groups of three shift workers, in the American Survey 56 per cent were dissatisfied; in the British group only 13 per cent. In the Dutch sample of shiftworkers 30 per cent were dissatisfied; but in the British study, if the results are to be believed, only 12 per

Table 5.1
Satisfaction with shiftwork or shift system. Percentage of workers

Attitude to shiftwork	AMERICAN SURVEY Continuous three shifts	DUTCH SURVEY Sample of all shiftworkers
Very favourable	3	10
Favourable	8	30
Neutral	33	30
Unfavourable	31	16
Very unfavourable	25	14
No of workers	225	493

Attitude to shift system	BRITISH SURVEY Continuous three shifts	Sample of all shiftworkers
Very satisfied	29	37
Moderately satisfied	57	50
Not very satisfied	9	10
Unsatisfied	4	2
Don't know, etc	1	1
No of Workers	180	619

cent were dissatisfied. There may be good reasons why the results from the surveys differ, eg they come from different countries or the questions asked were not worded the same, but it would be impossible to unravel the reasons for the differences. The fact remains that a reader of any one of the reports would go away with quite a different impression of the human aspects of shiftwork, than if he had read one of the other reports.

Asking the direct question – 'How satisfied are you with working shifts?' – is to oversimplify the issue and Maurice and Monteil may have obtained a truer picture by asking questions in two stages. In the first they asked 'Would you like to continue shift in the future or not?' The replies for continuous rotating three shift workers were:

Yes, without hesitation	32%
Yes, with hesitation	35%
No	33%

The men were than asked, 'On the assumption that your wages and work remain the same, would you prefer to do shiftwork or normal day work?' The replies for the same continuous shiftworkers were:

Prefer normal day work	63%
Prefer shiftwork	34%
No reply	3%

The answers to both questions showed that about one third of shiftworkers liked working on shifts and wished to continue to do so (on rotating two shift work two thirds of the workers felt like this). The main reasons given were habit (they were used to working shifts), the amount of time they had off and the financial benefit. About a third of the men said they wished to continue working shifts but with hesitation. These were people who did not really like shifts but were influenced by the extra money they could earn. When the second question was asked, which assumed that they got the same money on daywork, they opted to work on days. For many shiftworkers the choice is not a real one. They may live in

106

an area where employment is predominantly on shiftwork. They may join a company at a young age and start shiftwork; as length of service increases they acquire seniority and move on to higher paid jobs. In some process industries, such as iron and steel, there is a tradition that workers on senior production jobs are highly paid. If the man moved from shiftwork he could only command a much lower wage on an unskilled job on days. On the opposite side of the coin his family's expenditure has risen to match his earnings and to change to daywork would lead to a drop in living standards of a third or more. A proportion of shiftworkers are, therefore, compelled to carry on working shifts even though they may not particularly like it.

It is perhaps surprising that a third of continuous shiftworkers actively like the arrangement and would not change back to daywork if they had a realistic choice. Some social scientists are reluctant to accept this. They have argued that a favourable attitude to shiftwork is a rationalization which expresses the habituation of the shiftworker to his conditions but he is still alienated from the community. The argument is mistaken and does not sufficiently take into account individual differences between people, nor the importance of 'learning' to adjust in everyday life.

CHAPTER 6

Arranging the shift system

Once it has been decided to make greater use of the plant and equipment in a factory or if a review is made of an existing shift system then all the considerations discussed in the preceding chapters come into play. In arriving at decisions about shiftwork there needs to be an awareness of the biological background to it, of the social and cultural factors involved, of those factors which make for economic efficiency and high productivity, and of political events such as negotiated agreements, legal requirements and the effects of incomes policies. How far it is necessary to make an inventory of all these possible influences depends on the circumstances but many of them need to be considered and it is arguable that managers and workers should take more account of the biological background than they do at present.

In this chapter four central problems will be discussed: first, the adoption of double day or alternating day and night shift, second, the adoption of fixed or rotating shifts, third, the acceptability of shifts of longer duration, fourth, what to consider when arranging multiple shifts, eg stopping and starting times, direction of rotation.

DOUBLE DAY SHIFT OR ALTERNATING DAY AND NIGHT

In many countries both in Eastern and Western Europe

double day shift is more common than alternating day and night. In Britain the latter is more widespread and there are considerably more shiftworkers on day and night than double day. Many of the double day workers are women and if men only are counted the figures for selected firms, given below, show that there are more than five times as many men working alternating day and night shift than on double days. The information is taken from the survey of selected firms by the Industrial Society (1975). The results rest mainly on the motor vehicle industry where in the survey there were 35,808 men on alternating day/night shifts. (It is interesting to note that large numbers of motor vehicle workers may be feeling under par because of repeated spells of working at night.)

	Alternate day/night	Double day
Male	40,953 (5145)*	7881
Female	42	6845

*Excluding workers in the motor vehicle industry

The reasons for adopting alternate day and night shift were outlined in chapter 1 and are mainly concerned with the increased flexibility which this system gives to management to arrange production. Overtime may be worked on both the day shift and the night shifts, maintenance can be completed in between the shift changes and the size of the night shift can be varied so that fluctuating production needs are met. The standard hours of work are not generally reduced by a paid meal break, at least during the day, with the result that the increased costs of the night shifts are not so much greater as at first appears when compared to double day shift with paid meal breaks. Workers also accept alternate day and nightworking because of the extra earnings and some prefer a night shift to an afternoon shift with its disadvantages socially.

The repeated spells on night shift lead to the biological effects on the workers described in previous chapters. There is the constant need to adjust from a normal routine to working at night and resting by day. For some workers this results in difficulties in sleeping, adjusting to changed meal times and a general feeling of malaise. There is evidence that alternating day and night shift is the least preferred of the main rotating shift systems and there is the suggestion that fatigue accumulates on successive weeks of the night shifts. In view of these effects of alternating day and night shift and the possibility of choice between operating it and double day shift which sometimes arises, it is worth examining in some detail the merits and defects of the double day shift.

The double day shift consists normally of two shifts, a morning and an afternoon shift usually from 06.00 to 14.00 hours and from 14.00 to 22.00 hours but sometimes the shifts may start and finish up to an hour later, eg 07.00 – 15.00, 15.00 – 23.00. The more common earlier times are encouraged by the legal requirements regarding the working of abnormal hours by women and young persons and also the need to stop the late shift reasonably early in the evening to catch public transport home. Alternation of shift generally takes place weekly although sometimes the change takes place every day; one worker taking the afternoon shift of one day and the morning shift of the following day. Another method is to change over shifts in the middle of the week. Changing at more frequent intervals than a week means that some social and family life can be enjoyed at the normal times every week. The methods of change are illustrated below:

		Day of the week				
		Mon	Tue	Wed	Thurs	Fri
Shift	AM	A	B	A	B	A
	PM	B	A	B	A	B

OR

		Day of the week				
		Mon	Tue	Wed	Thurs	Fri
Shift	AM	A	A	B	B	B
	PM	B	B	A	A	A

The double day shift system was studied closely in the period between the two wars and immediately after the last war. Official interest took the form of two enquiries: the Departmental Committee on the employment of women and young persons on the two shift system which reported in 1935 and the Brierly Committee on double day shift working (1947). The Departmental Committee was set up to review the manning by women and young persons of double day shifts and the legal requirements, which are still largely extant. They accepted that women and young persons suffered few disadvantages from working this system and foresaw its wider adoption. The Brierly Committee was set up to see if the more widespread use of the double day shift would be economically beneficial and would be one method of improving industry's competitiveness. The Committee in its report took a very favourable view of the system and as a result the Ministry of Labour took steps to publicize the system, for instance by sending a letter to organizations of employers and workers in selected industries. The pressure has not been kept up but whether this is because the Department of Employment has revised its views is not known.

There has been some research concerning the working of the double day shift. The two government committees took evidence from a wide range of public bodies and from individuals, which is published in their reports. The Industrial Fatigue Research Board carried out an early study (Smith and Vernon, 1928) while a later survey has been conducted by Brown (1954). All the evidence points to the conclusion that after a period of adaptation those workers who remain on the system, both men and women, tend to like it and in many cases prefer the two shifts to daywork.

Brown (1959) interviewed 88 double day shift workers and of these 55 preferred double days to daywork. The system was more popular in firms which had operated the system for some time and less popular in firms where it had been recently introduced. Thus reinforcing the conclusion of the Brierly Committee that 'the reluctance to adapt to double day shift was based on an objection to the changes necessitated at the outset, and that the system was not unpopular with work people when they were accustomed to working it'.

Brown considered the difficulties of the double day shift for both men and women in relation to the shift worker himself/herself and its effects on the household. Married women find the double day shift more convenient than daywork for doing housework and shopping but more difficult from the point of view of looking after children. The housewife with young dependent children finds that arrangements work well if she manages to enlist the cooperation of her husband and relatives or neighbours who will help to look after the children. The difficulties encountered by the women seemed to depend on the stage of family development.

As regards the effects on the women shiftworkers themselves, they did not seem to be severe in most cases. The women did not complain of loss of sleep and lay in on the morning following an afternoon shift which compensated for any loss of sleep on the week of mornings. The shiftworkers did complain of feeling tired in the morning shift and some rested when they got home from the shift before starting housework. On the whole the hours of rest were longer on double day shift than ordinary daywork. Meal times were not so convenient on the morning shift. Many women had to get up at 5.00 am or earlier to get to work by 6.00 am and they did not have breakfast before they came in. As a result it was most important that a *break* was given *early* in the morning shift so that the shift workers could eat a breakfast that was provided either by the factory or by themselves bringing in their own food. They did not usually have a main meal in the middle of the day when they got home but waited until other members of the family returned from work. Meals on the afternoon shift presented no difficulties as it was possible to eat them at the normal time.

The social life of the married women appeared to be rather restricted and was confined to the weekend. There were not enough single women in Brown's sample for conclusions to be drawn but the evidence to the two government committees suggested that the afternoon shift was unpopular with young single women because it interfered with social life and courting. Therefore each shift had its advantages and disadvantages. The morning shift left the worker free in the afternoon and evening but it had the disadvantage of being tiring, allowing less sleep at night and displacing meal times. The afternoon shift was less tiring, the worker could do the housework in the morning, there were no difficulties over meals and she could lay-in in the morning. These were the advantages to older women workers. The afternoon shift was highly inconvenient socially both from the point of view of family life and social life outside the home and this affected the younger people most.

The men gave a more varied picture than the women and it was not so easy to generalize from the results but they are not basically different from the women's results. The shiftworker had about six hours in bed before the morning shift and nine hours after the afternoon shift. A few rested in the afternoon on their return from the more tiring morning shift; so over a cycle any sleep debt incurred was cancelled out. As with the women workers meal times were normal during the week of afternoons but presented difficulties on the morning shift. The need for an early break on the morning shift to allow for *breakfast* is worth emphasizing again. The shiftworkers' wives were put to some inconvenience through having to provide meals for their husbands at different times from the rest of the family. The effects on family life for many men were beneficial for they saw more of their wives – if they did not work – and more of their children below school age or on their school holidays. The shiftworker did not seem to become isolated but might develop a very close relationship with his family.

On the other hand there were severe social disadvantages on the afternoon shift, felt most by the younger men. The free time in the morning appeared to be wasted although it was appreciated by some who had hobbies such as fishing or even a spare time occupation such as small-holding and other married men liked to spend the time around the home and garden. To anyone who wanted social activities with friends or organized activities with clubs or societies, etc, the afternoon shift was a dead period. It was difficult if not impossible to become an office holder in an organization. The single

114

men particularly felt the week on afternoon shift as a social disaster and in one factory which had recently started shifts the investigator found a year later that most of the single men who disliked shift work had left. They found that they were cut off from their friends and could take little part in social life. The Departmental Committee (1935) had been concerned that the system would interfere with a young person's further education. Downie (1963) gave a gloomy account of double day shift working and it does appear that when this two shift system is introduced those who dislike it tend to leave. This is practical for the younger man but for the older man who has achieved some seniority in the factory it is a serious step for he would lose the benefits of his long service, such as higher pay and security. It is possible that the elderly worker can be on double day shift and be reluctant to move even if he dislikes it.

However the overall effects of double day shift are not too onerous except perhaps for the single person. The physical effects are slight and there is no evidence that the changed meal times lead to extensive digestive disturbance. Smith and Vernon (1928) compared sickness absence of double day shift and dayworkers. They found no difference in sickness absence experience although there was a greater amount of casual absences on the double day shift. These investigators found that the average hourly output was greater on double day shift but it was not sufficient to compensate for the greater output achieved through working longer hours on the day shift.

In conclusion double day shift has few serious drawbacks for the shiftworker (after all, daywork has its disadvantages!) and is not to be compared in this respect to shifts involving night work. It is perhaps surprising that attempts to encourage the use of the system have not led to its more widespread adoption.

Fixed or rotating shifts

The great majority of three shift workers rotate shifts over a cycle and most workers on two shifts alternate between day and night. There is no doubt that rotating shifts will continue as they are accepted and well-tried, nevertheless there are workers on fixed shifts and it is worth asking if they have any merit or if they warrant wider adoption.

The biological background to shiftwork has been discussed in previous chapters and an introduction given to some of the questions which experimental scientists are tackling in relation to circadian rhythms and phase changes in the sleep–waking cycle. It was noted that permanent nightworkers show some adaptation of rhythms but, in the everyday working situation, rarely a complete inversion at nights. Unlike people who make a complete change of environment such as the traveller by air and certain laboratory subjects – who do adapt – the nightworker retains some of his day time habits and is still subject to some normal social and domestic routines. The adaptation of the permanent nightworker is therefore imperfect but is more complete than the rotating shiftworker (Patkai *et al*, 1975). This has led some scientists to advocate, albeit cautiously, a long period on nights or permanent nights (Kleitman, 1963; Wilkinson, 1971) rather than rotating shifts. At present the scientists do not have enough evidence to make a very positive recommendation. Quite contrary to the notion of permanent nights has been the practice, fairly widely adopted, of rapidly rotating shifts (see pages 131) where workers may spend only two or three spells on one shift before changing to the next. There have been many more examples of these rapidly rotating shifts than of workers adopting fixed nights, although this does occur. The question is therefore fraught with difficulties.

It would be of great advantage if the night shift could be manned voluntarily. There are wide individual differences between people in their tolerance of nightwork and if from those who showed a certain adaptation there were sufficient willing to man the night shift, others who disliked nightwork or could not tolerate it physically would be left to man the corresponding day shift. An opportunity to study such an arrangement was afforded to De la Mare and Shimmin (1964) and De la Mare and Walker (1965, 1968).

This study was concerned with telegraphists who manned working stations throughout the twenty four hours. Jobs were generally interchangeable between staff and the men were allowed to work their preferred shifts by exchanging duties between themselves or to opt for a permanent night shift. The original rota was a variety of shifts in a complex 32 week cycle in which night duties were listed in every seven or eight weeks. One in five of all the listed duties were exchanged and 87 per cent of these changes were between day and night duties. In the original rota a man worked 25 to 35 per cent of his time on night shift. Figure 6.1 shows the number of men working different proportions of nightwork.

The results indicate that there was a preference for either permanent day work or permanent night work and few men chose to work mixed duties. These were arrangements freely entered into by the men concerned. The attraction of the permanent night shift in this case was unrelated to strict physiological adaptation because the night shift was an alternate one – a 12 hour night shift followed by a night off – and no physiological adaptation to a 48 hour living cycle has been demonstrated, but there were opportunities to adopt regular habits.

The investigators returned two years after the first study and found that the informal arrangements had been

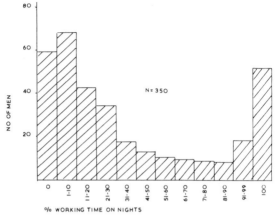

Figure 6.1
Distribution of population according to percentage time spent on night shift

From De la Mare G and Shimmin S, Preferred Patterns of Duty in a Flexible Shiftworking Situation, *Occupational Psychology*, 38, pp 203–214, 1961

regularized so that when an operator was promoted to a senior status he could opt for permanent days, rotating shifts or permanent nights. The majority choices showed even more polarization to regular day or regular night-work than before and the 951 operators were divided between the shifts as follows:

Perferring permanent days	60.9 per cent
Preferring rotating shifts	12.2 per cent
Preferring permanent nights	26.9 per cent

There was no difficulty in obtaining sufficient volunteers for the night shifts as there was, in fact, a waiting list to work for them. Interviews were held with small samples of men drawn randomly from those working on the three types of shifts. The stated reasons for their preferences are shown in Table 6.1 on pages 120–121.

Operators on all shifts found that they had useful free time but for rather different reasons. Thus the nightworkers appreciated that they had long breaks which allowed them to pursue outdoor hobbies during the day such as gardening or house improvements for their interests were largely home centred. The day shift which worked varied duties during the day liked having time off in the morning or the afternoon, as did those on rotating shifts. Thus the enjoyment of useful time off and long breaks was a feature of all three shifts.

The main reason for operators preferring the day shifts was that it got them off nightwork, which they found physically disturbing because it upset their sleep and their digestion. Many felt the night duty unduly tiring. The day workers' wives had disliked their husbands being away from home at night and leaving them alone in the house. The dayworkers also reacted to nights with general condemnatory remarks such as 'nights being unnatural' or 'I don't like the idea of nights'. The permanent nightworkers liked a number of features of their shifts: such as the ease of travelling, the quieter pace of work and less rushed atmosphere at nights; they found that they were used to the system and the regularity which it brought. Not many of them mentioned increased earnings but they were able to earn more at night particularly if they worked overtime. Those who preferred the rotating shifts gave very similar reasons for their preferences as the nightworkers except that they liked the variety of changing shifts compared to the preference for stability on the other two shifts.

The shiftworkers were also asked to show their attitudes to topics which might be affected by their hours of work by marking rating scales. The results showed that the nightworkers rated themselves very favourably on many social factors such as meeting friends, pursuing

119

Table 6.1
Reasons for preference

PERMANENT DAYS		ROTATING SHIFTS		PERMANENT NIGHTS	
Advantages	No of mentions (N=20)	Advantages	No of mentions (N=20)	Advantages	No of mentions (N=20)
Night work is bad for health — upsets sleep, eating, fatigue, too old	15	*Useful free time* weekends off, long break after nights	14	*Useful free time* long breaks between duties, free time during the day	17
My wife doesn't like me to work nights	9*	*Variety* night duty makes a pleasant change	9	*Travelling* including parking	12
Useful free time sometimes can lie in in the morning sometimes free afternoon	7	*Travelling*	6	*Regularity* know where you are, better for health	11

Travelling train service fits in well with duty times	7	*Used to it*	5	*Atmosphere on nights* companionship, quieter, less hectic	7
Nights unnatural don't like the idea of nights	5	*Shorter duties* due to night differential	5	*Used to it* set in ways	5
Regularity more regular hours of days, regular meal times	2	*Easy to arrange swaps*	4	*Money* overtime	4
		Stable pattern of duties no split duties	3	*Miscellaneous* including such highly personal reasons as freeing overcrowded sleeping accommodation	4

See same source as Figure 6.1

*out of 17 married

hobbies or enjoying their time off. Similarly they were able to enjoy family life and to attend to personal business, eg the dentist, haircuts, more easily than men on rotating shifts or varying day shifts. It may be that the favourable attitudes of nightworkers were defensive responses. On the other hand they did enjoy longer uninterrupted periods of time off, had higher earnings and a slightly higher standard of living. They even said that they had a better appetite and enjoyed their meals better. Records in self-completed diaries of when they ate showed that the nightworkers were able to establish more regular meal times than their opposite numbers on fluctuating shifts.

Four main influences were identified as contributing to the operatives' decisions as to which shift to work. The first was habit, once an operator had started to work a rota for one reason or another, eg to earn the night shift premium, he tended to adjust. Secondly, domestic factors were important. The dayworkers stressed the influence of their wives' dislike of night shift as determining their choice, while the nightworkers were well satisfied that the shift hours suited their domestic life, eg they could see more of their family. Thirdly, the physical effects of nightwork. The dayworker avoided nightwork because he felt it affected his health, upset his digestion, made sleeping difficult and led to fatigue. Fourthly, there was a difficult choice between financial reward and extra leisure. The former could be obtained at the expense of the latter by working longer shifts and doing overtime. Some preferred the free time, others with more responsibilities chose to work longer hours for the financial reward. One factor which was not related to the choice of shift work was personality, although a few night operators working little overtime were introverts who enjoyed the quieter working situation. In summary then, these shift workers freely chose their hours of work and were well adjusted to those they selected.

This kind of shiftwork is unusual, although sometimes men work a regular night shift while women work the double day shift. It is possible to visualize a fixed night shift (with consecutive rather than alternate night shifts) complemented by a double day shift. Fixed shifts during the day are impractical because of the unpopularity of the afternoon shift. These shift arrangements meet the physiologists' recommendation of allowing men to adapt, at least to some extent, to permanent nightwork, as it allows the development of stable habits, eg of eating and sleeping, denied to rotating shift workers. It permits men to reach their own balance between domestic, social and physical needs. Finally it establishes a flexibility which is absent from the arrangements for most shiftworkers but which is now being demanded by people at work.

ARE SHIFTS OF LONG DURATION ACCEPTABLE?

The surveys of shiftwork such as those by the Industrial Society (1975) and Sergean (1971) show that there are a large number of shift systems operated with shifts of longer duration than the usual eight hours. Ten or 12 hour shifts are quite common and 13 or 16 hour shifts have been noted. The total number of workers involved may not be great but it is increasing. The long shifts are associated with two main causes. The first relates to shifts on systems where a lot of regular overtime is worked and this is accomplished by extending the length of the shifts and long hours of work ensue as a result.

There are many ways by which overtime can result in long shifts. It may be normal day work with long extra hours, or by extending the shifts on alternating day and night shift in the time between the shift changes. Or extra long shifts may be added at a weekend; men may be brought in from rest days and others may work a double day shift of 16 hours as reliefs for absentees. A few factories still operate a three shift system with three crews each working a 56 hour week.

The second cause of long shifts is to work normal average weekly hours but to arrange the system so that it involves working 10 or 12 hour shifts. Two examples which are being increasingly adopted are firstly, the working of 4 × 10 hour night shifts, instead of 5 × 8 hour night shifts, in engineering factories and other firms, thus allowing a free Friday night on alternate day and nightwork or discontinuous three shift work; secondly, arranging a continuous three shift system with 12 hour shifts. For example the rota might involve working 4 × 12 hour shifts followed by four days off. The four day shifts alternating with four night shifts. The average hours of work are 42 a week. A variation of this is rapidly rotating 12 hour shifts. (Examples of the rotas are shown on page 130.)

Working abnormally long hours on a regular basis needs to be considered separately from the working of long shifts as part of a rota system with normal weekly hours of work. The effects of long hours of work were thoroughly researched in the First World War. In 1917 the Government was concerned about the fall in the output of munitions and appointed the Health of Munitions Workers Committee to investigate the reason. The committee found that factory staff were working up to 70 hours a week or longer and they proceeded to study the effects of these long hours. In a careful series of field investigations in industry the doctors and other scientists from the committee, later the Industrial Fatigue Research Board found, that productivity increased in inverse relation to the length of the working shifts. The lower the hours of work the higher the output per hour; there was
124

more produced in a 10 hour day than in a 12 hour day; measures of productivity showed increases on an eight hour shift and even on a six hour shift, although there comes a point where the increased productivity from the shorter shifts does not compensate for the drop in total output due to the shorter hours of work. One interesting feature of the studies was that after a shortening of the hours of work productivity did not rise immediately but did so gradually over a period of months till it stabilized itself at a new higher level. When hours of work were lengthened again productivity fell at once. The results of this work have been summarized by Vernon (1940). In a curious way history repeated itself in 1940 when after Dunkirk munition workers were asked to work excessively long hours; in a short term spurt output increased but it soon started to decline markedly and there was increased absenteeism but once the lessons of the First World War were pointed out the authorities reduced the hours of work. As a rule of thumb it has sometimes been suggested that staff can work a 48 hour week without any undue impairment of performance on all types of work except the most exacting.

Men who work long hours with extended shifts and overtime at the present day rarely reach the levels of hours of the munitions workers; but weekly hours of work between 50 and 60 hours is quite common and between 60 and 70 hours is by no means unknown. Surveys do not reveal that these hours are perceived as inefficient by management but opinions are no substitute for controlled study. The more exact and specific observations that can now be made on performance decrement which have been described in chapter 3 would make it possible to observe the effects of these long shifts more systematically. Nevertheless management can get by with them for a number of reasons. Lower paid workers welcome the long hours as a means of earning extra wages and often resist moving onto shorter hours. On automatic or semi-automatic processes which only require the intermittent attention of the operatives they work well below their capacity and can cope with fatigue so that it does not affect working performance. Over-manning may reduce the work load on workers so that they can tolerate the long hours. None of these reasons are particularly good ones for adopting shift systems with long hours. These systems are certainly undesirable where the work demands physical effort or continuous attention or is hazardous and it is doubtful if they really have a place in any type of work although they will probably continue in the old established workshop.

The working of long shifts, eg 12 hours, as part of a system averaging the normal weekly hours is quite another matter and it is worth considering this form of continuous shiftworking further because of its increasing popularity. An opportunity was presented for examining the reasons why some workers prefer long shifts in a study of an extended alternate night shift. The investigation was made some years ago when the hours of work were longer than now (Wyatt and Marriott, 1946, reported by Walker, 1961) but there is little doubt that much the same results are obtained today. The men were at work from 4.00 pm to 8.00 am for three 16 hour alternate night shifts in two weeks and worked from 8.00 am to 4.00 pm in the third week. This had replaced a more conventional three shift system. Most of the men expressed a stong preference for the long shifts. They liked the long break between shifts which provided more time at home and for social life. The second main reason for preferring the long shift was that it allowed for a long sleep so that a man went back in the next shift refreshed, whereas fatigue was felt to build up on successive night shifts. A remark made by one of the men illustrates the point:

> One of the many advantages of the 16 hour night shift is the social side and the time you get at home. I can now do quite a lot of things and can keep pace with friends, play games, take the kiddies out, or go to a show. I could not do these things on the three shift system because I didn't feel like it. Everything fits in better at home and things run very smoothly.

any adverse effects of long shifts require to be watched, they will depend on the nature of the work and the fitness of the individual. In the case of the 16 hour shift system quoted above a number of the operators had come off the long shift on grounds of health and others had reverted to the former three shift system at their own request. A more recent experimental study was carried out with nurses (Kogi *et al*, 1975) who monitored the performance of nurses working normal eight hour shifts and longer 12 and 16 hour shifts.

During the experimental periods night duties occurred twice per week and physiological measures were taken, such as pulse rate and temperature, in addition performance measures were recorded on such tasks as choice reaction and signal detection demanding continuous attention. On most of the bodily measures and tasks the results showed a lowering of function in the early hours of the morning on all shift systems, but the decrease was generally greater for the 16 hour shifts, intermediate for the 12 hour shifts and least for the eight hour shifts. The most pronounced decrease on the long shifts was in body temperature and performance on the tasks demanding sustained attention. The authors concluded that adjustment was poorer to the long night shifts although they point out that the long shifts did allow extended periods

127

for rest and leisure. In this experimental situation few of the nurses preferred the long shift although the study lasted for only a very limited period. It appeared that the inability of the nurses to rest before the long night shift and the active nature of the work contributed to the results. Kogi and his colleagues consider that it is most important to consider the work load before adopting long shifts, as well as social factors. However they concede that 12 hour shifts may be suitable for sedentary work as suggested by Colquhoun *et al* (1969). We would require a great deal more research on the effect of 12 hour shifts (as illustrated in table 6.2 on page 130) in the factory situation before any recommendation can be made. If the normal hours of work are not exceeded there are long periods of rest to recuperate from any fatigue that may have accumulated.

The evidence suggests that men are willing to work long hours in return for extended periods of rest and leisure. Working long shifts is one way of achieving this; another way is to work many shifts in a row and then take a long break. In one instance of computer staff that came to the author's attention, the operators worked 12 shifts successively and then had five days off. What is needed at present is a great deal more information on the effects of 12 hour shifts, particularly as they seem to be on the increase. For the present the manager can turn to the eminently sensible guidelines which have been suggested by Sergean (1971).

1 First, no one should be expected to work 12 hour shifts unless he chooses to do so . . .

2 Next, 12 hour shifts should only be used within the framework of the standard working week. It is comparatively easy to build overtime into this type of rota by bringing men in during their free time, but

this is a temptation to be avoided, except in extreme emergency . . .

3 Finally, as regards the type of work involved, shifts of long duration are not suitable for work having a heavy physical content, or of a continuous and monotonous nature, for example, many industrial inspection tasks. Nor are they advisable in jobs having a prominent danger factor, or in which exceptionally high standards of quality or purity are demanded. But for many types of lighter and more varied work they are worth serious consideration in view of their undoubted social advantages for those who have to work shift hours.

CONTINUOUS THREE SHIFT ROTAS

As the hours of work have been reduced so have three shift rotas changed. In the nineteenth century, 12 hour shifts were common. A major change and great social advance occurred at the end of the century when three crews manned the process plants continuously by working a 56 hour week, eg in the iron and steel industry. The rotas with these hours are simple ones because the 168 hours in the week is divisible by 56. As the hours of work were reduced through 48 to 44, the shift rotas changed and some of them were immensely complex, for instance, one 44 hour rota took 47 weeks to complete before the sequence of shifts started again. When the hours of work were reduced to 42, they were once more divisible into the 168 hours of the week and four crews provided a continuous coverage in a cycle of four weeks.

The rotas on a 42 hour week are simple to arrange and understand and provide regularity every four weeks which offers stability to the shiftworker and an opportunity to plan his activities outside work. Three of the main possibilities are illustrated in table 6.2 which

129

Table 6.2
Examples of continuous shift rotas (there are many variants)

Seven shift rota

Week	Day of the week						
	Mon	Tues	Wed	Thurs	Fri	Sat	Sun
1	M	M	M	M	M	M	M
2	off	off	A	A	A	A	A
3	A	A	off	off	N	N	N
4	N	N	N	N	off	off	off

$2 \times 2 \times 3$ shift rota

Week	Day of the week						
	Mon	Tues	Wed	Thurs	Fri	Sat	Sun
1	M	M	A	A	N	N	N
2	off	off	M	M	A	A	A
3	N	N	off	off	M	M	M
4	A	A	N	N	off	off	off

$2 \times 2 \times 3$ 12 hour shift rota

Week	Day of the week						
	Mon	Tues	Wed	Thurs	Fri	Sat	Sun
1	D	D	D	off	off	N	N
2	off	off	off	D	D	off	off
3	N	N	N	off	off	D	D
4	off	off	off	N	N	off	off

M = Morning
A = Afternoon
N = Night
D = Day

indicates the shifts that a shiftworker would attend in the four week cycle. The first is the conventional type of rota which has been traditionally worked in British industry, when each crew works seven shifts in a row, then has a two or three day rest break and moves on to work the next shift. The sequence of seven shifts may be shortened to six but the length of the rest periods are correspondingly reduced and the rota becomes much more complex. At present the normal hours of work are 40 but the length of the working week on these rotas is 42; the extra two hours can be paid at overtime rates or an extra day off can be allowed every four weeks or a week's leave after twenty weeks. Owing to its simplicity companies seem to prefer this type of rota to operating a rota averaging 40 hours a week which is possible but is much more complex.

The second rota illustrated is the so-called 'Continental' or 2 × 2 × 3 system which involves working two or three shifts in a row, having a 24 hour break between the change of shift, and a long break after six or seven shifts. A variant of this is the 'Metropolitan' or 2 × 2 × 2 system which is exactly the same except that only two shifts are worked in sequence followed by a long break of two days. The 2 × 2 × 2 cycle takes eight weeks to complete.

The third example is of a rota of 12 hour shifts. The rota may be arranged with any block of day and night shifts that are desired, the longer the sequence of 12 hour shifts the longer the corresponding breaks. Blocks of four shifts on followed by four shifts off are practised but a common variant is shown in table 6.2 including blocks of three shifts and two shifts. There are very many variations of shift rotas and if a rota is being designed reference can be made to the surveys periodically carried out by the British Institute of Management and the Industrial Society which detail the most popular rotas covered in the surveys. Another source is Powell (1966).

We have discussed the operation of rotas with shifts of long duration in the previous section noting the social advantages of the long breaks and the opportunity provided to recuperate, which must be set against the disadvantage of long tiring shifts which could, according to the type of work, affect performance.

The second main distinction between rotas, which are commonly worked, is the frequency of shift rotation; whether a crew works a long sequence of shifts, six or seven in a row before changing onto the next shift, or works two or three shifts before a change as in the 'Continental' or 'Metropolitan' rotas.

FREQUENCY OF SHIFT CHANGES ON CONTINUOUS WORK

The $2 \times 2 \times 3$ system was introduced into Great Britain in its present form in the late 1950s and 1960s, although swiftly rotating shift systems were not unknown and a $3 \times 3 \times 3$ system has been operated in the glass industry for many years. The swiftly changing systems were adopted, in the first instance, at the request of the workers and after they had convinced their managements that the systems were practical. This occurred in the chemical and iron and steel industries although the system has now spread widely. How well has it been functioning?

Studies have been made by Murrell (1965), Walker (1966) and Wedderburn (1967, 1975b). In one of these studies workers who had recently changed to a $2 \times 2 \times 3$ system or a $2 \times 2 \times 2$ system were interviewed and their attitudes to the new systems obtained, particularly in comparison to their previous systems which were of the more usual pattern with six or seven shifts worked in sequence. In both works the change had been at the men's request after they had voted in a ballot. The managements of both firms were not unresponsive to the wishes of their workers and agreed to work the systems on a trial basis when the position would be reviewed. However nothing further was heard of the reviews. 86 per cent of the men interviewed in the chemical works and all those in the Steel works preferred the new to the old systems although they had some reservations about the new systems.

There were two main reasons why the men preferred the frequent changes of shift. The first was physical. Both the morning shift, with the early start at 6.00 am, and the night shift were tiring for over the sequence of six or seven shifts on the old system it seemed to the men that fatigue built up and was not dissipated until after the long break, or the afternoon shifts when there was the opportunity to lie in bed in the morning. The number of hours of sleep before the morning shift averaged five to six, after the evening shift nine to 10 hours and after the night shift there was great variability, some men sleeping right through the day and others only sleeping a few hours in the morning. After both the morning and night shifts some men took naps in the afternoon thus increasing the amount of rest. The new rotas broke up the pattern of six or seven consecutive shifts so that there were only two or three of the tiring morning or night shifts in a row. The new system provided time for more rest and, at least subjectively, the men felt fitter and fresher. There is in fact ample time on this system for rest after an arduous shift as there is a 24 hour break between each shift and the easier afternoon shift followed the morning shift, similarly the long break provided time for recuperation after the night shift. Wedderburn (1967) suggests that 'swiftly rotating systems may have hit on an optimum solution for both the physiological and social needs of the man'. The review by Rutenfranz *et al* (1976) notes that if one shift is worked at night normal circadian rhythms are not affected. Perhaps even after two night shifts there is not too much disturbance.

The second main reason for preferring the rapidly changing rotas was that it reduced the monotony of six or seven shifts in a row. The changes meant that there was some free time in normal hours every week which gave an opportunity for social and leisure activity every week and the enjoyment of family life. More useful time off was a common remark when referring to the 2 × 2 × 3 or the 2 × 2 × 2 systems. On the long consecutive shifts the two weeks of afternoon and night shifts represented a 'dead fortnight' when the man could not enjoy pub or club, TV or radio or spend a complete evening at home. The breaking up of this period made it seem there was more time for leisure.

There were disadvantages to the new system for the length of the long breaks had been curtailed, particularly on the 2 × 2 × 2 system. Furthermore as the long breaks always started at 6.00 am after a night shift the men had to go to bed on the first day of their break which was further shortened. Also the morning shift followed the last day of the long break and the men had to be careful on the preceding evening so that they were prepared for the early start.

The 2 × 2 × 2 system was felt to be more satisfactory than the 2 × 2 × 3 system. One reason was that the latter was difficult to understand and some shiftworkers and their wives were confused as long as three years after the change of system. This underlines the need for each worker to be supplied with a shift calendar so that if he knows the date he can read his shift duty.

Management had expressed some doubts about the system in both firms. They thought that the new system would lead to difficulties of administration and communications between the shifts and between the shiftworkers and the day-time staff. Secondly, they were sceptical about any advantages accruing to the men from the rapid changes and the short breaks and thirdly, they feared a possible increase in absence. Management fears regarding difficulties of administration proved groundless as the following quotation from a company assessment shows:

> Management found it easier under the new system to keep in touch with shift workers and supervisors found it much easier to maintain more frequent contacts with shop stewards and works councillors. Fears that there would be a lack of continuity in running the plants proved groundless, as did fears of less effective liaison between the shift process supervisors and the day maintenance men who are mainly responsible for plant maintenance.

Management fears that the men would be disappointed also proved groundless but the possibility of increased absence is another matter.

A warning marker has been put up by Pocock *et al* (1972) who studied the absence of 782 shiftworkers for a period before they changed to a $2 \times 2 \times 3$ system and for a period afterwards. They found that the number of spells of sickness was 36 per cent greater in the year after the change compared to the year before and that the number of uncertified sickness absences increased by 29 per cent. There was no increase in casual absenteeism. However the post change period coincided with an influenza epidemic and the increase in absence might have been due to this reason. To check the possibility the authors compared the spells of sickness absence in the factory with the regional figures. Although the regional figures showed an increase between the two years it was much less than the increase among the $2 \times 2 \times 3$ shift workers. It is possible that the increase in spells of sickness was due to the new hours of work, although the validity of the study probably rests on whether the regional figures were a reasonable control with which to compare the shiftworkers' absence. It is important that this work shoud be repeated on a larger scale for this is the first indication that all may not be well in working rapidly rotating shifts.

Subject to the warning given as a result of this study the 'Continental' type of shift system works well, it presents few difficulties for management and is liked by the workers because it is socially advantageous and is felt to be less tiring. These two reasons are probably self sustaining for if the feelings of boredom are greater on traditional shift systems they will tend to reinforce any physical effects: if there is reduced 'fatigue' on the Continental system it would enhance the enjoyment of leisure. It is perhaps surprising that so few workers object to changing their living habits three times in the same week.

FREQUENCY OF SHIFT CHANGES ON THE TWO SHIFT SYSTEM

We have commented on the frequency of change on the double day shift and the continuous rotas involving 12 hour shifts in the appropriate sections. There remains the question of considering the changes on alternating day and night shifts. The most common period to change shifts is weekly but there are some companies where the changeover is made every fortnight and occasionally the change takes place monthly or at longer intervals. Sergean (1971) has surveyed the literature on this point and no agreement is found. When recourse is had to the shiftworkers own preferences they tend to prefer the system they are working on, although if there is an indication it is towards a shorter period on each shift, in the order of a week. The arguments for a weekly rotation are primarily on social grounds and the avoidance of boredom and 'fatigue' which come with a longer period on nights. The arguments for a long sequence of nights, say a month, are that some adaptation occurs to the shift. There is evidence that physiological adaptation is not complete even after a long period on nights although some modification of bodily functions, eg body temperature take place, but there is also the possibility that there is an adaptation of wider living habits, eg meal times which leads to a greater acceptability of the long period on nights. Unfortunately there is no agreement among the authorities on what is preferable, for they do not know, and asking shiftworkers for their preferences does not help greatly in deciding although the whole argument now seems rather old fashioned and has been overtaken by events.

The commonest method of changing is weekly with five × eight hour shifts on days and nights, but sometimes the staff work four × 10 hour shifts at nights and five × eight on days; although four × 10 hours may be worked on both days and nights leading to a four shift week of alternating day and night. The avoidance of Friday night shift on this system (and on permanent nights) is now common. On continuous work with 12 hour shifts it is not customary to work more than four shifts in a row which is quite arduous enough. The movement is towards a shorter period on each shift but the length of the shifts may be increased.

DIRECTION OF ROTATION

Changing the direction of rotation on continuous shifts can alter the distribution of time off on the long breaks. With the seven shift rota illustrated in table 6.2 there are three long breaks of equal length; 72 hours. The last long break of three complete days off at the weekend is in fact

137

no longer than the others and in terms of useful time is certainly no longer for the first day off starts at 6.00 am after a night shift and on the Sunday night the worker has to be ready for manning the morning shift on the Monday. By reversing the direction of rotation the length of the breaks becomes 56 hours, 56 hours and 104 hours. The long break is liked by some workers. Whether the long break is actually beneficial should be left to the workers to decide and a reversed rotation is sometimes requested by them. Similar considerations apply to the direction of rotation on discontinuous three shift systems where the length of the breaks vary according to whether they are forward or reversed. It is sometimes considered an advantage to have a long break after a night shift to allow for recuperation; although socially there is the disadvantage that the worker needs to sleep on the first day of the break.

STARTING AND STOPPING TIMES

The conventional shift times of 06.00 – 14.00, 14.00 – 22.00 and 22.00 – 06.00 hours are now being changed fairly rapidly to avoid the early morning start at 06.00. Starting at this time means a very early rise for a worker with any distance to travel. Shepherd and Walker (1956) showed in two steel works that three-quarters of the single shift absence occurred on the early morning shift and the other quarter was distributed more evenly over the other two shifts. It was suggested that the very large excess of single shift absence on the morning shift was due to the early start and the results of other studies tended to confirm this.

Single shift absence was found by the departmental managers and supervisors to be the most inconvenient because it was unexpected whereas it was possible to plan for longer term absentees through sickness. Many firms

138

now work shifts of 07.00 – 15.00, 15.00 – 23.00 and 23.00 – 07.00 hours or with a start sometime between 06.00 and 07.00 hours. As well as the effects of the early start on the workers with the possibility of oversleeping and the disruptive effect of the increased absence on the work there is also the problem of transport. It is becoming increasingly difficult to find transport home after a shift which stops at 23.00 hours. If the firm is large special buses may be arranged and the problem decreases as workers own their own form of transport. Another way of overcoming the difficulty is to increase the length of the night shift by half an hour or an hour and shorten the morning shift correspondingly; so the shift hours might be 07.00 – 14.00, 14.00 – 22.00 and 22.00 – 07.00 hours, thus avoiding both the difficulties of transport late at night and the early morning start. On the other hand it is doubtful if the best solution is to increase the length of the night shift which is already the most arduous shift.

Another solution is to introduce flexibility into the starting and stopping times so that men can arrange between themselves when to change shifts. Experience has shown that this can work well although occasionally there may be difficulty when a pair of workers cannot agree, or one of them is constantly late, and management may have to intervene. This must be set against the monitoring of lateness which also causes unpleasantness. It would seem more in keeping with the introduction of flexible working hours amongst other staff to permit shiftworkers a certain degree of flexibility in arranging their own starting and stopping times to suit their convenience, as it is of no consequence to supervision provided the job is covered. Flexibility in this context will probably come to be expected as a matter of course.

Recent trends

An indication of recent trends can be obtained from the Industrial Society's survey of shiftwork (1975) where 24 companies taking part in the survey had made changes in their shift rotas within the previous two or three years. There were many individual changes made by a single company to suit the workers or the needs of production but three changes were being adopted more generally:

Five companies changed the starting time of the morning shift from 06.00 to 07.00 hours.

Five companies changed from a traditional rotation after six or seven shifts to a $2 \times 2 \times 3$ or a $2 \times 2 \times 2$ system.

Four changed from five $\times$ eight hour shifts to four $\times$ 12 hour shifts. Concomitant with the change was the provision of extra rest days in three cases or the payment of overtime for the extra hours in one company.

As in most areas of working life change is rapidly taking place in the arrangement of shift hours. The adaptations discussed have taken place in response to many other changes; in for example the reduction of hours of work, in types of work, in social conditions. It must be expected that people will continue to experiment until they find rotas which are tolerable and which are sometimes preferred to day work. Two requirements seem to be a certain willingness to take risks and to keep the changes flexible so that there is room for choice. It would be advantageous if some examples of the changes that are taking place were monitored scientifically to discover features of the new systems which are acceptable and the pitfalls which should be avoided. It is highly unlikely that a single arrangement will ever be universally accepted for it is almost certain that companies will adopt the systems that are best suited to local conditions, for instance the type of work inside the factory or type of surroundings, urban or rural, outside.

CHAPTER 7

ଔଔଔଔଔଔଔଔଔଔଔ

The introduction and administration of shiftwork

The introduction of shiftwork leads to all pervasive effects upon the life of the shiftworker and his family. Some of the changes are beneficial but many cause inconvenience and a few lead to stress. All the changes are strange and many readjustments in working and family life are required. If a person is facing shiftwork for the first time it will be with some uneasiness and even fear, fed by folk tales and rumours about shiftwork and an imperfect understanding of what it involves. It is not surprising that managements who wish to introduce shiftwork are often faced by resistance to change and they need to exercise all the skills of communication, consultation and training to achieve a smooth changeover.

The problems will differ considerably according to the circumstances surrounding the change. If a type of shiftworking is being introduced in an area of the country where shiftworking is traditional or in an industry where it is generally worked then the change will be much simpler and meet less resistance than if it is introduced into a geographical area or industry where shiftworking is relatively unfamiliar. If there are technical reasons for introducing shiftwork which are absolutely clear to the worker then the grounds for opposing it will appear to him less convincing, but if the technical reasons are not clear and are not explained to him the changeover may appear capricious. Similarly there may be an economic need to introduce shiftwork which may not be immediately obvious to the man on the shop floor unless he is consulted in an open way. Wedderburn (1975b) after an exhaustive study of shiftwork in the British steel industry concluded that there are relatively few problems because these conditions, among others, applied in the industry.

The position will also differ according to the nature of the changes. Thus it will be different if shiftwork is introduced when a new factory or department is started and is manned by newly recruited staff, compared to the situation where the change is from one form of shiftworking to another in an existing plant. There are certain watersheds in the change to shiftworking of which perhaps the most important are:

(a) the change from daywork to two shift working
(b) a move to nightwork
(c) the change from two shift to three shift working
(d) the change from discontinuous to continuous three shift working.

Frequently the change to shiftworking is from daywork with long hours of overtime which makes for problems of negotiating the earnings of shiftworkers although the reduction in the hours of work which follow may make the change more acceptable. If the change is to a system involving working of a night shift for the first time, with all its disadvantages, its acceptance marks a hurdle which management and staff have to surmount. Similarly the change from two shift to discontinuous three shift working requires acceptance and adaptation to new rotas. The change from discontinuous to continuous working marks

143

an abrupt change from the weekend being free for all or most of the period to only having the occasional completely free weekend. This can be a real deprivation to men whose major social activities are reserved for the weekend.

To overcome resistance to the many changes which go with shiftwork thorough preparation is required involving a long run up to the change and extensive consultation and negotiation.

CONSULTATION

At an early stage in the decision making process the management will wish to consult with the workers representatives to inform them of the position. Acceptance is likely to be more readily forthcoming if the reasons for the change are apparent so that a full disclosure of the reasons for the change is desirable, notwithstanding that later bargaining will take place on the pecuniary compensation to shiftworkers when use will be made of the information disclosed. However the amount of premium is only one of the major issues and there are a whole complex of decisions that have to be taken in connection with the changes. Management and the unions might set up a joint steering group to see through the changes. The TUC (1973) has advocated that negotiations should cover all areas of decision about shiftworking and not just the narrow question of remuneration. Management will normally welcome this as consultation can help to iron out the difficulties attendant on introducing shiftwork. Other forms of consultation may also be needed such as works meetings with the staff where the position can be explained and discussed. If there is a crystallization of different opinions about some aspect of a shift system then a ballot may be taken to decide the issue. (In addition there is the legal requirement for balloting on

144

double day shifts when women and young persons are involved, see chapter 8.) Another useful safeguard is that the details of the shift system may be adopted for a trial period. This should be sufficiently long for adaptation to occur. As people on the whole come to prefer what they are used to only aspects of the scheme which are clearly unsatisfactory will be raised at the end of the trial period when there should be a review.

How the consultation and negotiation proceed will depend not so much on the nature of shiftworking but on the state of industrial relations in the company. If industrial relations are good and the need for shiftwork is apparent to all then negotiations will proceed in a constructive problem solving way. If relations are bad, negotiations will be difficult and their subject matter may not always relate to the problem in hand.

The first decision is on the amount of plant utilization required but once that is decided the management is not greatly concerned about the details provided the plant is manned for the required period. There are some other minimum requirements which management needs to see observed, for instance that a shift is not so long that it results in undue fatigue or that the shift changeover arrangements are such that there is an orderly handover of work without friction. But most arrangements can be worked out in consultation with staff. These choices were discussed in the last chapter but they bear repeating again and when planning a continuous three shift system include:

the hours to be covered by the system
the average weekly hours to be worked
the choice of fixed or rotating shifts
the form of the rota
the number of shifts to be worked between rest pauses

145

the length and distribution of rest pauses
the frequency of shift changes
the direction of rotation
the starting and stopping times of the shifts
the length of shift.

The arrangements of shift rotas in an industry or a locality or in a company have often arisen through practice and are adopted through habit so that the question of choices has never been faced; for example, the conventional starting time of the morning shift on continuous work at 6.00 am is thought to have originated many years ago when alternating 12 hour shifts were worked, although a later start is worth considering. In firms which have worked shifts for a long time the reasons for adopting particular arrangements are often historical ones and once work-people have operated one system they adapt to it and either do not wish to change or have never considered doing so. The adoption of the so-called Continental system (eg $2 \times 2 \times 3$ or $2 \times 2 \times 2$ systems) which occurred frequently in certain areas during the 1960s is an example of a spontaneous change of customary shift rotas. The working of a four shift $\times$ 10 hours at nights instead of a five shift $\times$ eight hours is another example of a change which grew from the shop floor. Despite these alterations to common practice shiftworkers are slow to make a change.

There are a number of ways of enlarging the range of choices, all of which require building into the arrangements a degree of flexibility. It is possible to permit and even encourage the exchange of shifts between workers when it is desired for social or domestic reasons. There can be flexible starting and stopping times so that members of the different crews change over at times to suit their convenience which avoids the monitoring of lateness. This was discussed in the last chapter. Similarly there can be flexibility in the type of shift rotas worked in different departments to suit the wishes of staff. Small groups of workers on shifts can make their own arrangements under supervision. Wedderburn (1975b) showed in the steel industry that workers who were not able to exchange shifts or vary their shift times by arrangement with other workers were more dissatisfied with shiftwork than those who could.

There are individual differences in people's preferences and in their ability to adapt to shifts. If a variety of systems co-exist in a factory it will be found that workers gradually select themselves onto the type of system which is suitable for them. It does not seem to be good practice for a company with different factories throughout the country to lay down standard shift arrangements but rather to let each site make its own arrangements to suit the traditions of the locality and the wishes of the staff. Research on shiftworking has not reached the stage when it can prescribe the optimum arrangement for shift hours and in fact may never be able to do so.

This flexibility may sound disorganized or even anarchic but it is a recognition of what already exists. Sergean (1971) draws attention to the variety of shift systems that obtain, often on the same site, and how they evolve and change even though habit is a powerful stabilizing influence. He writes:

The greater the choice of rotas and the more varied the alternation, the easier it is for the employee to fit in with company planning. Flexibility in arrangement of hours helps individual adaptation. The principles of consultation and choice, variety and flexibility, must involve additional administrative chores for the company, but these are likely to be repaid in terms of improved employee morale. This morale derives in part from the satisfaction that comes from participating in a scheme which one has helped to devise oneself. Secondly, from a sense of acquiring some degree of control over the way in which one's hours at work and hours away from work are arranged.

It is not always possible to meet the wishes of the staff who may sometimes plan unsuitable hours of work, eg excessively long night shifts, and technical conditions may determine the arrangements. Nevertheless flexibility should be built into a system whenever possible although the arrangements should not go unsupervised, for if that occurs unacceptable practices can develop. Perhaps the term 'controlled flexibility' is appropriate. To maintain this employers will need to write into the staff's contracts of employment that working shifts is a condition of employment thus ensuring that operational needs can be met.

The Advisory Conciliation and Arbitration Service (ACAS) (1976) in a paper draws attention to yet one more reason for consultation.

> In recent years, Industrial Tribunals have heard a number of unfair dismissal cases in which an employee has not accepted a change in shiftworking arrangements and has either been dismissed as a result or has resigned claiming 'constructive' dismissal. In considering whether the employer has acted reasonably in these cases the Tribunals have taken into account whether, and how much, consultation and discussion took place with employees and employee representatives before the changes were implemented.

Employers will wish to consult their employees through their representatives, to do so early in the planning stage and to conduct thorough negotiations. It is possible that as they proceed employers will find themselves increas-

148

ingly bargaining over a wide range of matters connected with the intoduction of shiftwork.

COMMUNICATIONS

One of the most persistent difficulties associated with shiftwork is maintaining effective communications. There is a tendency for shiftworkers to become isolated from the main stream of factory life. Just as in their social life they may become isolated from their friends and the community, so at work they may become isolated from other staff. This occurs most for permanent nightworkers who may never be in the factory at the same time as the day shift, except briefly at shift changeover time, but difficulties of communication may arise on any type of shiftwork. The attitudes which the day shift has towards the nightworker illustrates the point. In one organization with a permanent night shift when staff were being interviewed during a research study (de la Mare and Walker, 1968) the permanent day shift workers told the investigators to wait until they met the night shift who were 'queer people' and 'pale like ghosts'. When the permanent night staff were interviewed they looked healthy and sunburnt from the outdoor hobbies they pursued during the day such as gardening and golf. Further when their scores on a personality test were compared with the day workers' scores, they were found to be about the same and remarkably close to the norms for the population as a whole. If myths grow up about shiftworkers among day workers, the former also react to the situation. The crews on shiftwork may develop into very close 'in-groups' even to the extent of resenting the outsider so that friction may develop between them and the day shift or between the shift crews themselves.

The problem seems to have three aspects. First, to ensure that the shifts are adequately supervised and managed. Second, to see that there is good liaison between shifts. Third, to see that the shiftworkers are provided adequately with the services which are part of normal life in the factory during the day. Communications are important in all three areas.

Information and orders may not be transmitted accurately to shift crews or even be passed down at all from the departmental management and more particularly from top management. It is possible to communicate by written instruction and memoranda, but although these may supplement oral instructions they are not an adequate substitute for face-to-face communication. The highest representative of management on shifts is frequently the foreman who will be the main intermediary between shift crews and management. Whenever the numbers justify it good practice is to appoint a shift manager but it is rarely the case that on three shift work supervision should be multiplied by three, for there are many activities that are carried out by day which are not practised during the evening or at night. There is no point in employing shift managers or supervisors who are underemployed during the night. A balance has to be struck between providing thorough supervision during shift hours and wasteful duplication. If communications are to be maintained so that information about production or technical matters is provided for shift supervisors and shift managers, then they should be expected to come into the factory by day at some time during the week when there are meetings to attend. Conversely senior management and certainly the departmental manager should pay visits to the factory during the early evening and occasionally at night to see that all is well on the production side and to deal with any individual problems.

The same kind of considerations apply to workers'

representatives who should have opportunities outside shift hours to attend at the factory for meetings during the day. Shiftworkers may tend to be overlooked in industrial relations affairs and the trade union representatives may lose touch for it is difficult for them to find out what is going on. If managers, supervisors and trade union representatives are expected to attend the factory outside their own working hours then they should be compensated by time off in lieu and/or additional remuneration. Even the senior manager if he is expected to attend the factory at night on some occasions should receive a tangible reward otherwise the duties may be performed reluctantly and it will seem to those concerned that they are doing one-and-a-half person's work for one person's pay.

The second type of communication failure may occur between the crews on different shifts. At the time of shift changeovers the outgoing crew will be eager to leave work and the handover may be somewhat perfunctory. The keeping of written records or log books is one way of passing on information. They may be a useful method of communication provided they do not replace personal contact. A short period of overlap when both crews are on at the same time may be practical. Certainly the supervisors, and if present, the shift managers should ensure an orderly handover including a short period of overlap. Another method is for the shift supervisors to meet during the day sometime in the week or to meet on a Sunday.

Sometimes friction develops between shifts and when this occurs it should be tackled at an early stage. One possible cause of friction is the method of paying shifts. Where there is an incentive scheme such as a group bonus the question arises as to whether to pay the shifts together as one group or to pay separate bonuses to the shifts. If

151

each shift receives its own bonus the incentive effect may be sharper than if the shifts are paid together. There is evidence that output tends to decline the larger the size of the payment group. On the other hand paying the shifts as one may encourage the crews to pull together while paying the shifts separately, although it may increase the incentive effect, can cause the shift crews to pull in different directions. As illustration the case of the foundry may be cited where so many 'heats' are completed in a furnace during a shift. If a 'heat' was completed shortly before the end of the shift the furnaceman did not bother to start to prepare the furnace for the next 'heat' for if it was not completed before the end of the shift no bonus would accrue to him, but to the furnaceman on the next shift. If the shifts were paid together then it would be to the furnacemen's mutual advantage to keep the work flowing continuously. Management and work-people will need to give careful consideration to the merits of paying the shifts separately or together. Account needs to be taken of the degree of dependence of one crew on another; if this seems substantial then it is better to pay the shifts as a whole to encourage teamwork but if the shifts operate relatively independently then paying bonus earnings separately is the most suitable.

Some organizations in recent years have introduced 'briefing' groups to improve communications. In this system small groups of managers are 'briefed' by their superiors on policy and information which requires to be conveyed down the line. Each manager then goes and 'briefs' a group of his subordinates and so on until all are informed on the shop floor. Information is sometimes said to 'cascade' down the organization by means of communication between overlapping groups. Over-lapping in the sense that a member of one group is also a member of one or more other groups. 'Cascade' is a singularly inept expression to describe the transmission which should occur for it only flows one way – downwards. Effective communication is a two-way process and if any system is employed such as 'briefing' groups it is essential to see that feedback is passed up the line as well as information passing down. Part of the problem of the isolation of shiftworkers is their feelings that their views are not taken into account and their opinions are not heard. Management will wish to establish and maintain two-way communication with shiftworkers.

SUPERVISION AND MANAGEMENT

Attention has been directed to the difficulties of maintaining supervisory and management cover at night. Managers may be none too keen to take up shiftwork for a number of reasons other than the usual disadvantages of shiftwork. In communities where shiftwork is rare it is considered somewhat *infra dig* to work when others are enjoying their leisure so that it is not socially acceptable. This feeling applies more sharply to managers from the middle class but perhaps less to the working class more of whose members work shifts. The shift manager may also find that his position in the organization lies outside the normal career structure and his career development can be impaired. He will need some reassurance.

Supervisors, foremen and charge hands occupy key positions particularly if there is no shift manager. They have to shoulder more responsibility and will have to cope with production problems and staff difficulties on their own which would normally be handled by more senior staff. Some foremen welcome the added load but others find it too much. If shiftworkers are employed in any number additional training should be given to shift supervisors. These, like the managers, may feel that their promotion chances are reduced because talent goes unrecognized on shiftwork. The difficulties will be felt less if the managers' and supervisors' shift allowance are relatively of the same order as the staff they supervise. Thus the wage differential between the shift supervisor and his day time equivalent should be as large as the differential between the shop floor shiftworker and dayworker. This will help to attract the able supervisor as well as compensating him for the inconvenience of shiftwork.

In summary the supervisor on shifts, especially on nights, has a more arduous job than his counterpart on days, for he has to keep in touch with day time activities in the factory and maintain good communications: he takes on more responsibility for the work owing to the absence of management and supporting services and looks after many personnel matters of his staff. To do all this effectively he must be of the right calibre, adequately trained and rewarded. Perhaps most important of all he must receive the necessary support and encouragement from his senior managers.

RECRUITMENT AND SELECTION

Recruitment of shiftworkers can be a problem. The difficulty can be the shortage of recruits willing to work shifts or recruiting the right mix of skills to man the plant. Both aspects can be more acute in an area where shiftworking is not the accepted pattern of work and few are willing to come forward to work unusual hours. Some methods of recruitment can ease the problem. For example if a new plant can be phased in then recruits can be obtained over a period. They can be trained and settled in stages without having to try and recruit at one time staff for the whole factory. If it is an extension to an existing plant or a changeover to shiftwork then new recruits may be engaged in the initial stages and when the existing staff see them adjusting to shifts they too may be willing to become shiftworkers. Similarly older staff may be more willing to move to shifts if they have already seen other workers in the plant adapting to rotating shifts. Labour turnover may also be a problem when shifts are first introduced because those who do not wish to work them leave. However surveys show that this does not generally remain a problem once shifts have been operating for some time, although problems of labour turnover may continue among certain kinds of shiftworker such as part-time married women (Ministry of Labour, 1967).

It would be easier to recruit shiftworkers if management knew the kind of person who would adapt most readily to shifts, who would be most likely to stay, and also the person who would be unlikely to adjust. If there were physiological measures available which could select out those who could not tolerate the disturbance of bodily functions from shiftwork they could be excluded. However these measures do not as yet exist. There are some guidelines as to who might be rejected at any pre-employment medical examination. For instance Aanonsen (1964) considers that people who suffer from peptic ulcer or other gastro-intestinal disorders may be excluded from shiftwork; similarly people with nervous disorders if the symptoms are pronounced; so too should workers who have difficulty in sleeping. But he goes on to add that the nature of the work, adequate opportunities for sleeping and the ability of the person to adapt to shiftwork rhythms are all important so that there are no disease conditions which positively counterindicate shiftwork.

The attitude of the shiftworker seems to be of great importance for in Aanonsen's study a substantial proportion (more than a third) of workers who suffered from nervous and gastro-intestinal disorders preferred shiftwork to day work. However there are certain major disorders which are thought to counterindicate shiftwork.

155

These include heart conditions, high blood pressure, epilepsy and diabetes. Those with chronic bronchitis would be better on day work largely because of arduous travelling conditions in all weathers late at night and in the early morning. It is also probably undesirable to start elderly men on night work for the first time in their lives.

Another guide to the recruitment of shiftworkers is to identify people who would be likely to be attracted to shiftwork and to remain on it. Some clues are provided by examining the effects of the incentives to work shifts. If shiftworkers are classified by the amount of their financial responsibilities it is found that those with heavy responsibilities tend to work on shifts. A measure of family responsibilities which is associated with financial commitments is the income tax code number of the worker as allocated by the authorities in the Inland Revenue. It has been shown that at the status level of the factory worker the tax code number is a good indication of marital state and number of dependants. Even when a man's tax number takes into account other commitments such as an allowance for the interest on a house mortgage it is still possible to take the income tax code number as a measure of domestic financial responsibilities.

Walker and de la Mare (1971) selected groups of men on permanent night shift and day shift in three quite different organizations. They were then divided into income tax code groups to correspond to single men, married, married with one child, married with two children and married with three or more children. The results in table 7.1 show the numbers of men on night shift and day shift in the different groups. It is seen that there are fewer single men and married men with no children on the night shift than on the day shift, but a greater number of men with four or more dependants on the night shift.

A similar investigation has been made by Fishwick and

Table 7.1
Number of men in different tax code groups on day shift
and night shift

ITC groups	No of dependants					Total
	0	1	2	3	4 or more	
Day shift	125	187	124	84	55	575
Night shift	86	148	117	100	128	579

Harling (1974) who compared the proportion of workers on shiftwork and daywork grouped by age and domestic responsibilities. The large samples of men were from firms in the British motor car industry and a Belgian plant. When the shiftworkers were grouped by age there were a greater proportion of shiftworkers than dayworkers aged in their late twenties, thirties and early forties. The dayworkers tended to be disproportionately represented among the young and the old. When the workers were grouped according to domestic responsibilities as measured by tax code number the pattern was very similar to that found in table 7.1. There was a greater proportion of shiftworkers among those with heavy domestic reponsibilities broadly corresponding to three or more dependants and a greater proportion of dayworkers among those with low domestic responsibilities broadly representing single men and married men without children.

As age and the amount of domestic responsibilities in a population are related it is not possible to say that age and tax code differences separately identify differences between shiftworkers and dayworkers. The authors took the analysis a step further. They selected a group of men with common tax codes and examined what relation there was between shiftwork and age. The previous relationship still held. Similarly they selected a group of men in the same age group and examined the relationship between tax code and shiftwork. Again the previous relationship held. Thus both age and domestic responsibilities are independently related to shiftwork.

It is interesting to speculate why shiftworkers compared to dayworkers should show particular characteristics of age and domestic responsibilities. So far as the latter is concerned the influence of financial rewards may be paramount, men with more dependants to support need the money. But the age relationship seems to be due to other reasons and the very young and older men may avoid shiftwork for different reasons. Speculatively it might be suggested that the young value their leisure hours at the normal times, whilst the older men may avoid shiftwork because they find it tiring and stressful. Whatever the reasons the recruiting officer will need to take note and have it in the back of his mind that many men in the middle age range with domestic responsibilities make good bets as shiftworkers but he should not take any positive action for shiftworkers are drawn from the full age range and with the full range of family responsibilities.

Training

Training will be required for newly recruited shiftworkers whose performance needs to be of a high standard to cope with the added responsibilities on night shift. The Ministry of Labour survey on the introduction of shiftwork (1967) found that in the firms surveyed there was considerable redeployment from daywork to shiftwork and in two thirds of the firms there was a requirement for additional workers. As there were real problems of finding staff with the right skills, training programmes were even more necessary. They were easier to mount when the recruitment was phased. In one case where there was unphased recruitment machine efficiency dropped from 80 per cent to 68 per cent. Although training usually takes place on the day shift instances of training on double day shift have been reported. This draws attention to the point that on-the-job training, which is a feature of day work, often cannot be provided at night.

In addition to job related training, opportunity should be made for the Industrial Medical Officer or, if suitable, the State Registered Nurse to give a talk to workers facing shiftwork for the first time. This talk might outline the effects on bodily rhythms of nightwork so that staff have some appreciation of the reasons for the effects which it may have on them, pointing out the importance of setting time aside for sleep and attention to regular habits of elimination. Perhaps most emphasis could be given to the diet of shiftworkers which often consists mainly of sandwiches and tea in the workshop when there is the need for a balanced diet eaten under reasonably hygienic conditions. If the shift rota on which the new recruit is to work is at all complicated then it should be explained to him. Finally another short talk could deal with personnel arrangements so that the new shiftworker knows to whom he can take personal problems, pay queries, etc. If an induction course is held it would not be quite the same for shiftworkers as dayworkers but take into account the matters outlined.

MAINTENANCE AND OTHER SERVICES

Just as there is the problem of deciding what supervision to provide in the evening and at night so decisions have to be made about ancillary and maintenance workers. There is a balance to be struck between leaving the night shift unsupported which is inefficient and providing services which are underemployed which is equally inefficient.

This applies to such people as toolroom staff, maintenance workers and inspectors.

On most types of shiftwork it is possible to carry out maintenance at normal times or to make provision for it to be done outside shift hours. For example on double day shift maintenance can be carried out at night and on alternating day and night shift it can be completed in the breaks between the shift changeovers in the evening or early morning. On discontinuous three shift work it is possible to do maintenance at the weekend. All this does involve high labour costs with shift premia and overtime.

The greatest problem arises on continuous three shift work when down time for maintenance is expensive or technically difficult. Management will keep to the schedules of planned maintenance suitable for the plant and equipment but it is also possible to practise some self-help. If there is a breakdown in one section of the plant which stops production on other sections it provides an opportunity to carry out maintenance outside the planned schedule with all available staff. In this way production may be maintained at a higher level of efficiency. When service cover, such as maintenance or inspection, is not provided at night the day time crews when they start work will need to make good any deficiencies. They must be alert to the maintenance needs which are sometimes ignored on the night shift.

ADMINISTRATIVE FAILURE

It is instructive to quote from the Ministry of Labour survey (1967) the administrative reasons for failure to establish shiftwork in some of the firms they covered:

1 Lack of adequate planning in the early stages. In one firm shiftworking was introduced during a major reorganization of management

2 Lack of adequate consultation. Although the introduction of shiftwork had received official trade
union backing, consultations with shop-floor workers were skimped. The workers voted decisively, in
secret ballot, against shiftwork

3 Failure to study the local labour market in advance.
In one area where unemployment was low and
plenty of evening work was available, it was found
impossible to recruit women for an afternoon shift.
The firm had not informed itself of this position
beforehand

4 The false assumption that young people would be
prepared to forego evening and weekend leisure for
the sake of increased pay

5 Lack of planning on the production side. In one firm
modern machinery was introduced into the section
without adequate steps being taken to improve the
capacity of other departments to deal with the
increased output.

SHIFTWORK ALLOWANCES

Trade unionists and others often put forward the argument that the sole incentive to work shifts is the pecuniary
reward in the form of shiftwork premia and allowances.
They require to be large enough to attract people onto
shifts, to make it worth their while to stay on shifts and to
provide an equitable return for the inconveniences and
even hardships of shiftworking. Evidence presented earlier in this chapter that men with high family responsibilities are more likely to work shifts than those whose
commitments are lighter gives support to this view. To
management the increased labour costs are the largest
additional outgoing which will have to be met as a result
of adopting shiftwork or changing from one form of
shiftwork to another. Both groups, management and

workers, have a critical interest in the amount of the shiftwork premia and allowances.

The total amount paid in shift allowances is therefore of great importance. Negotiated rates are itemized in publications of the Department of Employment (1976), Confederation of British Industry (1976) and occasional studies by Incomes Data Services (1973, 1975). Some indication of the amount paid in shift allowances is obtained by considering the percentage addition to wage rates. The National Board for Prices and Incomes (1971) suggested that continuous three shift systems led to an addition to the labour costs of a third and double day shift led to a one-sixth increase. The Confederation of British Industry (1976) have calculated the percentage increase to the total wage rate of workers on continuous shiftwork. They have done this for a representative unskilled job, usually a labourer, and for a skilled job, usually a craftsman, in a number of industries. The usefulness of these figures is enhanced because they include weekend premium rates, commonly paid at time and a half or double time, according to the period of the weekend worked. The results in 10 industries show that for the unskilled the average (mean) percentage shift-worker's weekly rate of the day worker's rate was an additional 42 per cent with a range of 23 per cent to 63 per cent according to the industry.

For nine industries the craftsman's shiftwork weekly rate was on average 37 per cent greater than the equivalent day wage rate with a range of 19 per cent to 64 per cent. The lower average difference for the skilled, 37 per cent as compared to 42 per cent for the unskilled probably reflects the influence of flat fixed rate allowance, where paid, which will have a greater effect on the labourers low wage than the craftsman's higher wage. One other set of figures has been produced by Sergean and his colleagues
162

(1969) for shift payments as a percentage of the minimum hourly rate of pay. These exclude overtime payments, eg at the weekend, and as a result continuous shiftwork is omitted. The investigators analysed a large number of negotiated agreements and determined that the shift payments as a percentage of the minimum hourly rate of pay were:

Permanent nights	24.7%	range 7.5% to 50.0%
Discontinuous three shift	14.9%	range 2.0% to 29.7%
Double days	12.2%	range 2.0% to 33.3%

These figures probably give a good indication of the relative payments on the three types of shiftwork but not a good picture of the absolute differentials between shiftwork and day work.

For a number of reasons all the figures quoted must be treated with caution as percentage increases in rates can be misleading as an indicator of shiftwork differentials. In the first place the standard hours of work may be less (or more) for shiftworkers and in some cases may include paid meal breaks. Secondly there is no common method of calculating the hourly or weekly wage rates used as a basis for calculating the shiftwork allowances between industries or occupations, eg bonus and cost of living allowances may be consolidated in some instances but not in others. Thirdly, shiftworkers may receive additional overtime payments at the weekend and sometimes at night which must be taken into account in any comparison with day work.

There are a variety of ways of paying shiftwork premiums and the CBI report (1976) lists the following:

1 Differential basic rates of wages, higher for shiftworkers than for dayworkers

2 Flat-rate allowances, per hour, shift or week, additional to the daywork rates

3 Fixed percentage additions to the day work rates

4 Extra allowances for weekend shifts forming part of the normal working week

5 Payment at premium rates for normal hours worked by shiftworkers outside, or in excess of, the normal daily or weekly hours of dayworkers

6 An additional payment for hours worked between 8.00 pm and 6.00 am and/or for any hours worked on Saturdays, Sundays or public holidays.

For any industry or indeed any factory, as rates are often negotiated locally, more than one method may be used for paying the premium. This has important implications for the method of paying wages. If the weekly pay is based on the actual hours that are worked in the week there may be wide discrepancies in the shiftworkers' take-home pay in different weeks of the shift cycle. For example the wage will be high in a week when the shiftworkers have manned shifts over the whole of the weekend and it will be low on the morning shift during the week without overtime payment. As workers and their wives find fluctuations in weekly earnings inconvenient the choice of arranging the shift cycle is limited by the need for the weekly wage to be broadly the same on each week of the cycle. An alternative method of overcoming fluctuations in wages from week to week and at the same time not restricting the way the shift system is organized is to pool the allowances for the shift cycle and divide them evenly over the weeks. In this way one weekend may be left entirely free, a social advantage, without resulting in low wages because the hours worked attract no overtime payment. If this practice is adopted a check needs to be kept on the absence figures for unpopular shifts, eg Sunday afternoon or nights.

Despite the variety of allowances they can be divided

broadly into two types: those which are a flat rate, equal for all, eg 10p per hour, and those which are a proportion of the basic hourly (weekly) rate, eg time and a half. Sergean (1971) divides the shift systems he dealt with in analysing collective agreements into those paid on a fixed rate and those which were paid on a proportional basis with the following results.

	Fixed method	Proportional method	Total
Permanent nights	31 (26%)	87 (74%)	118 (100%)
Three shift discontinuous	37 (66%)	19 (34%)	56 (100%)
Double days	39 (56%)	32 (44%)	71 (100%)

The table above shows that more of the permanent night systems were paid by the proportional method but more of the three shift systems and the double day systems were paid by fixed methods. It is not possible to say why this occurred.

With proportional methods the shift premiums are automatically uprated whereas the fixed method of paying the shift premiums may mean that they are not adjusted when new rates are negotiated. This is no doubt one reason why Sergean showed that payments by the fixed method were lower than by the proportional method; for instance the average (mean) value of premiums for permanent night systems were 26.7 per cent by the proportional method compared to 16.4 per cent by the fixed method and there were, similarly, differences with the discontinuous three shift and double day shift systems. This automatic uprating of the shift allowance with the proportional method is of advantage to the workers in ensuring that the differentials between shiftwork and daywork are maintained. On the other hand it is sometimes argued that it is inequitable for the higher paid workers to receive proportionately more than the lower paid by way of a recompense for the inconvenience of working shifts. This is suffered equally by all and the rewards should be similarly shared so that a fixed premium seems fairer.

In addition to the shiftwork premiums some negotiated agreements provide for the situation where a shiftworker has to change between shiftwork and daywork or to change from one type of shiftwork to another on a lower rate of pay. The agreements usually provide that adequate notice should be given of the change or that a compensatory payment should be made if the notice is not given. Employers may also undertake to compensate for a time any drop in earnings which follows a change.

The question arises whether the premia paid for the different types of shiftwork are a fair recompense and whether the differences in the premia between different shift systems are equitable. There are no answers to these questions. Sergean *et al* (1969) suggested that social, psychological and physiological measurements might be developed which would provide a scale of inconvenience of different shift systems which could be used as a yardstick to determine the financial reward. This seems optimistic and another point of view is that the amount of the premia should be left to the market place and a fair reward is an amount which would attract and hold shiftworkers in sufficient numbers. The shift systems which were least preferred would in this way carry the highest premia. In practice the premia will reflect among other things the amount necessary to attract labour, the amount the industry can afford to pay and has historically paid and the relative bargaining power of trade unions and managements. The trade unions will have as one of the factors uppermost in their minds the inconvenience caused to the worker and are anxious to be able to quantify the costs and any benefits to him. The range of premia paid for the same shift system has been quoted earlier in the chapter and is so wide that it demonstrates that there is no single influence on their determination. The relative (mean) position of the premia (25 per cent for permanent nights, 15 per cent for discontinuous three shifts and 12 per cent for double days: see page 163) seem to represent rough justice in that they correspond approximately to the number of hours worked outside the usual day work times on the three types of shift system. If however night work is rated as causing the greatest inconvenience then discontinuous three shift work seems undervalued.

In considering why people work shifts the financial reward is clearly the most important reason but there are other compensations which are meaningful to some shiftworkers. The shorter hours with paid meal breaks may attract. Having time off for leisure during the day at different times of the week than normal allows for recreation and hobbies which could not be pursued so actively on day work. It has been suggested that these kinds of benefits to shiftworkers could be extended, for example, longer holidays or early retirement. When asked large numbers of shiftworkers prefer shiftwork to day-work not only for financial reasons.

Other ways of improving the shiftworker's lot are to provide extra facilities for his benefit such as repeating popular TV programmes in the mornings or extending licensing hours. A shiftworker may decide to work shifts because he has a financial need, eg saving up a deposit for a house, but when this has been accomplished he finds that he develops new needs which require fulfilment – a young family, the wish to buy a new car. In this way when the original reasons for earning and spending the money from shift payments disappears a new need arises. It has been said 'l'appétit vient en mangeant'. Habit is also a powerful reason for a man continuing on shiftwork once he has started it. Thus the reasons for working shifts are complex and many dimensional even though the financial reward is paramount.

This reward has been affected by the incomes policies of Governments over the last few years. Stage II of the Conservative government's incomes policy, 1972–73, led to the increase of wages which were at the expense of shiftwork differentials. This was even more pronounced in years one and two of the Labour government's wages policies, 1975–77, stage III of the Conservative government's policy went against the trend and introduced the concept of 'unsocial hours'. These were defined as hours worked between 8.00 pm and 6.00 am and any hours worked on Saturdays, Sundays or Public Holidays. These hours could attract a premium of time and a fifth and encouragement was given for a large number of claims to be settled. But on the whole incomes policies so far in the nineteen-seventies have led to a narrowing of differentials between shiftworkers and dayworkers and the undermining of the value of the shiftwork premia. The author of a report from Incomes Data Services (1975) points out that when resources are invested in industry then the workers must be there to use them. Many of the people will have to work on shifts and will expect to be adequately recompensed. He concludes:

> In those industries and companies where shiftworking is of paramount importance, and for those employees whose pay packets include an additional payment for the hours they work, a more sophisticated incomes policy that takes account of their special requirements and expectations will be something the architects of incomes policies cannot afford to overlook.

168

оооооооооооо

Welfare and legal aspects

WELFARE ASPECTS

The provision of welfare arrangements for shiftworkers is not on the same scale as for dayworkers and the shiftworkers are not usually provided with the full services. This was demonstrated in the Dunlop Company (Windle *et al*, 1969) where a survey was carried out of the proportions (per cent) of dayworkers and nightworkers who benefited from the following services provided by the company.

	Day workers	*Night workers*
Canteen	98%	37%
Specially arranged transport	47%	60%
Doctor or nurse available	89%	68%
Total numbers of workers	18,237	8254

This shows that provision of full medical cover was less for the nightworkers than the dayworkers and many fewer of the former enjoyed canteen services. On the other hand special transport was more frequently laid on for nightworkers than dayworkers due to the shifts starting and stopping at inconvenient hours. These results are broadly similar to the results of other more extensive surveys. The reasons for the lower provision of services at night are partly economic in that they are extremely expensive to provide particularly on the night shift which is invariably smaller than the full day shift, but another reason is that the services when provided are often not extensively used, eg the canteen. It is therefore not cost effective to give parity of treatment to nightworkers. However there is evidence that in some respects their needs are not fully met and the subject warrants further discussion.

CANTEENS

The issue of providing canteens is not simple for where they are open they are well used by workers on the morning shift, but advantage is taken of an open canteen less frequently on the afternoon and night shifts. Attention has already been drawn to the failure of workers on an early morning shift to eat a breakfast before they come into work. It is therefore essential to arrange for a meal break early in the shift. The early research of the Health of Munitions Workers Committee (1917) demonstrated that productivity was less in the quarter shift before the meal break and, although this research has not been repeated more recently, workers cannot be expected to give of their best before a breakfast early in the morning. On the afternoon shift it is customary for men to have a main meal at midday before they come in for the shift. While on the night shift many, probably most workers, do not feel inclined to eat a large cooked meal in the middle of the night. The eating habits of shiftworkers, as well as the high cost of staffing a canteen, lead to the provision of facilities which are less than a full canteen service as table 8.1 shows. The figures are drawn from the Industrial Society's survey (1975).

In the companies, where there is no canteen cover at night, there may be a mess room with facilities for heating

Table 8.1

The numbers and proportions of companies offering facilities for meals

	Shiftworkers		Dayworkers	
	No of Companies	%	No of Companies	%
Full canteen facilities	59	42	119	86
Vending machine only	30	22	8	6
Cooking facilities or facilities for heating pre-prepared food	36	26	7	5
No facilities	14	10	5	3
TOTAL	139	100	139	100

From Industrial Society, *Survey of Shiftworking Practices*, Survey No 94, 1976

food or vending machines. The report of the National Board for Prices and Incomes (1971) states that:

> about 60 per cent of workers on night shift had no canteen facilities – though snacks or the means of warming food might be provided – but about half the nightworkers with access to canteens did not make use of them.

It is customary in many parts of the country for shift-workers to bring in their own food usually in the form of sandwiches or pies (often called a 'piece' or 'bait') which is eaten in the mess room or, where this is not provided, in the workshop. The conditions are often unhygienic, for instance in a mechanized foundry the author watched the workers heating the water for their tea and heating their food on the hot metal castings on the conveyor. It is also questionable whether the food brought in by the workers meets high dietary standards. These facts give grounds for believing that some of the gastro-intestinal disorders from which nightworkers are prone to suffer may be due to the unhygienic conditions in which they eat unsuitable food. There might be considerable short-term gains if some practical research was carried out on the dietary needs of nightworkers and advice for them prepared.

TRANSPORT

It is often necessary to arrange for special transport for shiftworkers at the beginning and end of shifts. The Industrial Society's survey found that about a fifth of the companies surveyed made special transport arrangements for shiftworkers but about the same proportion also did so for dayworkers. There are usually no special difficulties in enlisting the help of transport companies provided the numbers of shiftworkers are sufficient to warrant the extra transport. This raises difficulties as increasing numbers of shiftworkers provide their own transport and thus opt out of any special arrangements.

Another way of meeting transport difficulties is to alter the time of the early morning shift from the traditional time of 06.00 hours to 06.30 or 07.00. This is a common change. On the other hand if the shifts remain of eight hours duration the afternoon shift will stop of 22.30 or 23.00 which is late for local transport. A common solution is to change over from the afternoon shift to the night shift at 22.00 hours as is usual, but to make the night shift half-an-hour or an hour longer – not an ideal solution as it adds to the length of the most arduous shift. In practice, outside strictly urban areas, people will be increasingly expected to supply their own transport.

Medical and first aid arrangements

Some larger companies provide a fully equipped surgery with a nurse in attendance at night. In other cases medical cover at nights is provided by a surgery serving a number of factories on an industrial estate. In most cases the surgery is covered by night staff who go about their normal work but are on call and who are trained first aiders; or where there is no surgery there will be a first aid box with foremen or others trained in first aid available in case of need. There are statutory obligations on the provision of medical facilities.

The appointed factory doctor or the industrial medical officer, if one is employed, does not as a rule provide cover at night except perhaps to be on call in case of an emergency. He does have another role, in assisting in the selection of shiftworkers who are starting work for the first time, on giving advice to shiftworkers who experience illness which makes them unsuitable for continuing shifts, or giving more general advice to shiftworkers on diet and other adjustments in living habits which shiftworkers have to make (see page 159).

Welfare

Other welfare arrangements are not usually supplied at night and workers are expected to come into the factory by day to attend to any problem or queries they may have, for instance personal problems or pay queries. The shift foreman may act as an intermediary between the nightworker and day-time services. But it is useful for the night nurse or some other appointed person to be known as the reference point in the first instance for welfare queries, for if there is not an accepted channel of communication then personal problems may be neglected.

Few companies provide social facilities for their shiftworkers. If a large firm has a works club it may be opened at times during the day for shiftworkers or occasionally a dance is arranged but on the whole shiftworkers are left to their own devices in this respect. Some crews are very active in organizing social events for the shift such as a football or darts team or arrranging outings. Nevertheless the general expectation is that the shiftworker will arrange his social life to fit the pattern of his day-time living. Many shiftworkers do strive to do this so that meal times and time for recreation conform to normal living as closely as their hours of work allow; the result is an uneasy compromise. The question may be asked as to whether the community can do anything to improve the shiftworkers' lot.

WELFARE OF SHIFTWORKERS OUTSIDE THE FACTORY

Suggestions have been made from time to time (eg Downie, 1963) that the community should sponsor recreation and other facilities for shiftworkers outside the hours which they are normally provided. Sometimes the suggestions show little awareness of the reality of the situation for instance that shops or doctor's surgeries should be open at certain hours for shiftworkers. This is unnecessary for the shiftworker is free at hours during the day which enable him to shop or attend to personal business, such as visiting the barber, the dentist or the doctor's surgery. He is in a better position to do these things at normal times than dayworkers, particularly if the dayworkers work on overtime. But as has been shown in chapter 5 the shiftworker is at a disadvantage in keeping up with friends, in attending organized social activities or participating in clubs, societies or adult education. He finds it difficult to be a member of a club committee or take part in trade union or political activity.

These are real disadvantages felt most by the young but they apply to any shiftworker who wants to take part in community life.

The steps that the community can take to alleviate the problem are limited. In most areas shiftworkers are thin on the ground and even in a shiftworking area, as in a 'steel town', only a quarter or at most a half of shift-workers will be free at any one time. One crew will be working, one will be resting, a third will have to be ready for the next shift and only the fourth will be fully free. With double day shift women workers regard the hours highly suitable for combining paid work with running a house, so that it is unlikely that many of them would want to take part in organized social activities during the day. In shiftworking areas it may be possible to do something such as having working men's clubs open during the day for the benefit of shiftworkers. It might be practical to run educational classes during the day in popular subjects, such as car maintenance, to suit shiftworkers and other minority groups who are free during the day, eg the elderly. Of course educational facilities during term time are fully used during the day and there is little spare capacity. Another possibility is to repeat popular television programmes during the morning for the benefit of shiftworkers and others. This might be practical but it does not do much to bring shiftworkers into community life.

Another suggestion which has been put forward is that a sound-proof room should be constructed in shift-workers' homes so that they might enjoy undisturbed sleep during the day. Attention has already been drawn to the difficulties which shiftworkers have in obtaining day-time sleep. Sleep is often disturbed by day-time noise and even when the shiftworker is asleep there is some evidence that the quality of his sleep is affected by noise.

It might not be too costly to provide a sound-proof room in the shiftworker's house. The problem is to isolate the room both from noise outside the house and also from noise inside the home, from children or from the noise of housework. New building materials and techniques make sound-proofing easier, for example double glazing insulates against noise. Consideration might be given to provide some financial help for the shiftworker to insulate a room in his home, so that he could improve the chances of obtaining sound sleep during the day.

Up to the present the community has spent few resources, if any, to meet the special needs of shiftworkers. There is scope to do something, but the solution to the problem of the social isolation among shiftworkers may lie elsewhere than supplying special facilities for shiftworkers. Some workers are now on a compressed working week of four shifts and if this trend continues they will be joined by many others; the shiftworkers' hours of work may shorten further so that the problem is less acute. Shiftworkers who adjust well often take up activities such as golf, fishing or an allotment which are day-time activities but they tend to be solitary or pursued by small groups. Any democratic community must express some concern if large numbers of its members are partially excluded from taking part in institutional life.

LEGAL ASPECTS

The hours of women of 18 years and over and of young persons (those over the compulsory school age but who have not yet reached the age of 18) in industrial employment are subject to legal restrictions. There are in general no similar restrictions for men, excluding some industrial groups, eg shop workers and bakers as it is deemed that men or their trade unions can look after their own interests.

176

The legislation relating to hours of women and young persons employed in industry consists mainly of Part VI of the Factories Act (1961) together with the Hours of Employment (Conventions) Act 1936 and the Employment of Women, Young Persons and Children Act 1920. These govern the hours of work of women and young persons in factories and control the total hours worked. Exclusive of intervals allowed for meals and rest, these should not exceed nine in any day, nor 48 in any week. A period of employment in a factory working a six-day week shall not exceed 11 hours in any day and shall not begin earlier than 07.00 hours nor end later than 18.00 hours in the case of young persons who have not reached 16 years, or in other cases, 20.00 hours, or 13.00 hours on a Saturday. An exception is made in any factory operating the five-day week as the total hours worked in any day may extend to 10 and the period of employment in any day may extend to 12 hours.

Similarly a start may be authorized earlier than 07.00 hours but not earlier than 06.00 hours. Legal rules are also laid down for the length of the breaks, in that women or young persons shall not be employed for a spell of more than four and a half hours without a break of at least half-an-hour for a meal or rest but if a 10 minute interval is allowed the period before a half-hour break may be extended to five hours. There are exceptions to these rules in that authorization can be obtained to increase the hours for young persons under certain circumstances; and overtime is permitted for women and young persons, but legally limited to a specified upper limit. For example a factory working a five-day week may also employ women and young persons on a Saturday, provided the total hours overtime worked do not exceed four and a half and no other overtime is worked in a week. The employer also has to display a notice of the hours of work and can only vary them after due notice.

These provisions of the Act are subject to certain exceptions if authorized by The Health and Safety Executive (HSE). Amongst them are authorizations for shiftworking.

SHIFTWORK FOR WOMEN AND YOUNG PERSONS

The HSE can authorize the employment for an indefinite period of women and young persons over 16 years of age on a system of shifts with the times specified on the authorization. A shift shall not begin earlier than 06.00 hours nor end later than 22.00 hours (14.00 hours on Saturday). The average hours of each shift must not exceed eight hours but if there is no work on Saturdays then the hours of each shift must not exceed 10 hours in a day, nor 48 hours in a week, nor 88 hours in a fortnight.

Before the HSE will authorize shiftwork for an indefinite period, provision has to be made for consulting the work-people and this will be by secret ballot to ensure that a majority of those concerned consent to working these hours. The conditions for consultation and the holding of the ballot are described by the British Institute of Management (BIM) (1965):

> Before the Minister will authorize the introduction of shiftworking for women and young persons the work-people concerned must be consulted in accordance with the Shift System in Factories and Workshops (Consultation of Work People) Order 1936. (S R and O, 1936, No 1367). The Order requires a secret ballot of all the work-people concerned in order to ascertain whether or not the majority of them are in favour of shiftwork. The occupier must inform the work-people concerned of the reasons for instituting the system and he must post a notice at the entrance to the factory in a conspicuous place and in any part of the factory where

these work-people concerned are employed giving information on the following points:–

1 Process or departments in which the shift system is proposed
2 Hours of work and meals for each shift
3 Arrangements for alteration of shifts
4 Adjustments in wages and working conditions
5 Other relevant information
6 Time and place at which the secret ballot will be held.

The ballot must be conducted jointly by the occupier and a representative chosen by the work-people. Details of the conduct of the ballot are set out in the Order. Any disagreement over the provisions of the Order or the arrangements for the ballot must be referred to the District Inspector of Factories who may, if he thinks fit, conduct the ballot himself. . . .

If a factory is recently established and the working of the system of shifts is intended to be permanent the authorization can be granted without consultation or ballot. If the application is for a temporary period of emergency an authorization may be issued but it will not be issued or extended beyond six months. The HSE can insist on conditions which it considers necessary for the purposes of safe-guarding the welfare and the interests of the work-people concerned, with particular regard to the provision of suitable accommodation for clothing, of the facilities for meals, of transport facilities and for young persons reasonable facilities for attending courses of further education.

Revocation of the authorization for shiftwork may be made by the HSE if the legal conditions have not been complied with or abuses taken place. The employer is required to notify the discontinuance and any subsequent resumption of shiftworking. If the shift system has not been in operation for 24 months the authorization is automatically revoked and it may be revoked by the HSE after a 12 month lapse in operating shifts. The HSE may authorize shiftworking for any period up to 12 months without the necessity for a ballot under the special exemption order procedure.

SHIFTWORK FOR MALE YOUNG PERSONS IN CERTAIN INDUSTRIES

If a male young person works in an industry which, because of the nature of the process, has to work continuously the terms of the Act vary from the conditions outlined above. The young persons may end a turn on Sunday morning not later than 06.00 or begin on Sunday evening not earlier than 22.00 hours and if they work on a four shift system with not more than eight hours on each term they may work between 0.600 hours and 22.00 hours on Sunday. But the number of turns in a week shall not exceed six, the interval between turns must not be less than 14 hours and two or more consecutive weeks of night shift must not be worked, although these conditions do not necessarily apply to the glass industry. The total weekly hours shall not exceed 56 nor 144 in any continuous period of three weeks.

The industries and processes are:

the smelting of iron ore
the manufacture of wrought iron, steel or tin-plate
processes in which reverberatory or regenerative furnaces are necessarily kept in operation day and night in order to avoid waste of material and fuel, are used in connection with the smelting of ores, metal rolling, forges or the manufacture of metal tubes or rods, or in connection with other such classes of work as may be specified by regulation of the Minister

the galvanizing of sheet metal or wire (except the
  pickling process)
the manufacture of paper
the manufacture of glass.

There are many exceptions to the Act of which two
general ones are relevant to shiftwork. Factory legislation regulating the employment of women does not
apply to those who are in responsible management positions and who do not normally engage in manual work,
nor to women employed solely in cleaning the factory.
Similarly Part VI of the Factories Act does not apply to
male young persons employed as part of the regular
maintenance staff of a factory or by a contractor, in
repairing any part of the factory or any machinery or
plant therein. There are other exceptions to the Act and a
procedure is laid down for employers to notify them to
the Inspectorate and to the work-people concerned. These
complex provisions are summarized in a booklet published by HMSO on behalf of the HSE, *Hours of
employment of women and young persons*. The Factory
Inspectorate is always willing to give advice and should
be consulted in any case of doubt.

SPECIAL EXEMPTIONS

Special exemption orders may be granted by the HSE
from the restrictions on employment in industry of
women and young persons aged 16 and over, subject to
certain conditions, on application to the Factory Inspectorate. Orders are valid for up to one year although the
exemptions may be extended if further applications are
made. Renewal is not automatic. The employer must
apply in writing and the HSE carefully review each
application before reaching a decision. Whenever any
significant change in the circumstances has taken place

the factory is again visited and the views of all parties concerned are ascertained. Table 8.2 shows the number of workers affected by exemption orders for various reasons in August 1976 (*Department of Employment Gazette*). The reasons are concerned with exceptions to hours of work laid down in the Act for women and young persons. The numbers seem relatively small, adding up to just over 200,000 women in all and a very small number

Table 8.2

Employment of women and young persons exemption orders, August 1976

Types of employment permitted by the orders	Women 18 years and over	
Extended hours*	24,256	
Double day shifts†	44,018	
Long spells	10,398	In addition,
Night shifts	48,964	14,913 young
Part-time work‡	21,336	persons between
Saturday afternoon work	3,784	16 – 18 years old were affected
Sunday work	47,117	by special
Miscellaneous	4,753	exemption orders
TOTAL	204,626	

* 'Extended hours' are those worked in excess of the limitations imposed by the Factories Act for daily hours or overtime.

† Includes some women employed on shift systems involving work on Sundays or on Saturday afternoons, but not included under these headings.

‡ Part-time work outside the hours of employment allowed by the Factories Act.

Adapted from the *Department of Employment Gazette*, 1976.

of young persons. One interesting feature from the point of view of shiftwork is that the HSE is willing to authorize women to work night shifts. The numbers so authorized are still not large but have been growing.

In addition to these special exemption orders for individual factories, made by the HSE, the Secretary of State may make general exemption regulations covering industry as a whole, or a section of industry, where application is made by a joint industrial council, a wages council, a conciliation board or 'other similar body constituted by organizations which appear to be representative respectively of the workers and employers concerned'. The Secretary of State may also do so on application by an organization which appears to be representative of the employers or workers concerned, after consulting the corresponding organization representing the other side of the industry, or on a joint application by such organizations representing the two sides. The term 'organization' includes in this connection an association of trade unions (eg the Trades Union Congress) or of employers' organizations (eg the Confederation of British Industry). The regulations when made take the form of a statutory instrument which must be laid down before Parliament for approval, and if approved, published.

EFFECTS OF OTHER LEGISLATION

Other legislation has been having its effect on shiftworking practice and employers and trade unions need to keep abreast of events so that they do not make mistakes or lose benefits. Some of the legislative effects have been identified by Incomes Data Services (1975).

The method of calculating redundancy pay for shiftworkers is one such problem. It is based on the average of the shiftworker's last 12 weeks if he has worked hours on days of the week or at times of the day which vary from week to week, so that his pay varied accordingly. To calculate the shiftworker's redundancy pay, the average weekly hours are multiplied by the hourly rate of remuneration. The former figure is the average normal weekly hours over the previous 12 weeks. Normal weekly hours refers to the standard hours the employee has contracted to work. Overtime is not counted unless 'the employer is bound to provide overtime and the employee is bound to work it'.

A second effect of legislation is the problem of unfair dismissal. There have been cases of employees being discharged, or they have resigned and claimed 'constructive' dismissal because they refused to work shifts or refused to change from one shift system to another. One of the features of the case that the tribunals took into account was the amount of consultation there was between management and the workers' representatives before the changes took place. Employers can write into the terms of the contract of employment that working shift rotas is a condition of employment with the company and thus obtain some protection.

A third important area is concerned with the Equal Pay Act as amended by the Sex Discrimination Act. It has been a practice to employ women on double day shift but to maintain a three shift system by having the night shift and Sunday shifts (if worked) manned by men who are paid at a higher rate than the women. The Employment Appeal Tribunal (as reported in the *Times*, 29 October 1976) has decided that in a case of this kind night shift work by men is broadly of a similar nature. The terms of the Act state that:

> a woman is to be regarded as employed on like work with men if, but only if, her work and theirs is of the same or of broadly similar nature and the differences (if any) between the things she does and the things they do

are not of practical importance in relation to terms and conditions of employment, and accordingly in comparing her work with theirs regard shall be had to the frequency or otherwise with which any such differences occur in practice as well as to the nature and extent of the difference.

The Appeal Tribunal concluded that 'the mere time at which work was performed' did not constitute a difference between the men's and the women's work sufficient to merit a difference in pay.

Review by the Equal Opportunities Commission

The question of the removal of the protective restrictions on the employment of women in factories has been the subject of long standing controversy. Some people regard these restrictions as discriminatory, denying women the opportunities open to men to earn more money by working overtime or at night. On the other hand others maintain that this legislation is protective and in accordance with current practice in many advanced industrial societies; and also that, because women tend to be less well organized than men, it protects them from undue pressure by employers to work long hours.

The Sex Discrimination Act 1975 does not alter legislation regulating the hours of employment of women. The Government felt it would not be right to remove the restrictions without consideration of all the arguments and all the possible consequences. Provision has therefore been made, under Section 55 of the Sex Discrimination Act, to require the Equal Opportunities Commission, in consultation with the Health and Safety Commission, to review legislation dealing with health and safety at work which requires men and women to be treated differently. The review will include legislation which regulates the hours of employment of women. The Secretary of State has, in fact, asked the Equal Opportunities Commission to complete a first review by the end of 1978. It will be for the Equal Opportunities Commission, if it so decides, to make proposals to the Secretary of State for any amendments to the legislation.

INTERNATIONAL ASPECTS

Each country has its own legislation about hours of work and some prescribe the maximum number of hours with provisions for exemptions. These laws are usually partly bound by the conventions of the International Labour Organization (ILO), for the member states who have ratified them and for some of them who have not. The aim of ILO standards relevant to night shift has been primarily to protect women and young persons from employment on shifts. The two areas of most concern are standards relating to night work and standards relating to the length and distribution of the main weekly rest breaks, specifically Sunday work.

Limitations on nightwork which relate to women and young people are contained in Nightwork (Women) Convention (Revised), 1948 (No 89) and Nightwork of Young Persons (Industry) Convention (Revised) 1948 (No 90). The former, the convention for women defines 'night' as:

a period of at least 11 consecutive hours, including an interval prescribed by a competent authority of at least seven consecutive hours falling between 10 o'clock in the evening and seven o'clock in the morning. Women without distinction of age shall not be employed during the night in any public or private industrial undertaking or in any branch thereof, other than in an undertaking in which only members of the family are employed.

The convention for young persons is similar. It prescribes nightwork for young persons under 16 years of age for a period of at least 12 consecutive hours which shall include the hours between 22.00 hours and 06.00 hours. For young persons aged from 16 to under 18, 'night' still signifies a period of at least 12 consecutive hours but will include an interval of at least seven consecutive hours, falling between 22.00 hours and 07.00 hours. The competent authority can prescribe different intervals according to the employment, but is required to consult the employers' and workers' organizations if work begins after 22.00 hours. For the purposes of apprenticeship or vocational training in industries or occupations which are required to be carried out continuously the competent authority may, after consultation with the employers' and workers' organizations concerned, authorize the employment of young persons, over 16 and under 18, on nightwork. If this occurs a period of at least 13 consecutive hours between two working periods shall be granted.

Neither of these conventions have been ratified by the UK because of the policy to permit employment at night of women and young persons in certain circumstances. In other respects the British legislation keeps to the spirit of the convention.

A fairly recent discussion of the problem in the UK is in a report (1969) of a working party, mainly composed of representatives from the CBI and the TUC, set up by the Department of Employment and Productivity which considered whether any changes in the legislation of hours of employment of women and young persons were desirable. The working party did not agree on many points but it did recommend some relaxation of the legal requirements regarding the hours of work of women although it was not specific as to what these should be. It considered that nightwork was unsuitable for all female young persons and also for most male young persons, except in certain continuous process industries. The working party also considered that nightwork was unsuitable for women in most instances and adopted the definition of 'night' quoted above from International Labour Convention No 89. Maurice (1975) summarizes the legal provisions for women and young persons with respect to shiftworking in EEC countries.

A second area of interest is the legal requirements surrounding the weekly rest-break in certain countries. In accordance with the standards and recommendations of the ILO, many countries provide for a statutory period of rest of 24 hours in a week and in principle the ILO conventions suggest that the rest day should coincide with the established traditions and customs of the country or district: in the EEC this involves Sunday as a rest day. Legislation about the rest day in EEC countries has taken one of two directions. Sunday is the legally designated rest day in Belgium, Holland and West Germany with provisions for exemptions. Where these occur they emphasize the need to keep as many free Sundays as is possible. In France and Italy the rest-day involving a 24 hour break can be taken on any day of the week provided it occurs weekly. Where stress is laid on a Sunday break consideration is being given to preserving religious life as well as family and social life. As shiftworkers value their free time at the weekends when they can take part in normal social activities, attempts to preserve a free Sunday should not be dismissed lightly. In the UK there are no regulations on hours of work for men (excluding certain groups such as shopworkers and bakers). Employers are 'penalized' for Sunday work by having to pay high premium rates and the unions press for these rates partly as a recompense to staff but also to discourage employers from adopting weekend work. Women and young persons are protected from having to work on Sundays except in certain circumstances, as has been discussed.

To conclude this section on the legal aspects of shiftwork, there is increasingly a greater intrusion of the law into the conditions surrounding shiftwork. This is not so much direct legislation on shiftwork, for in this respect there has been little change in the law and what change there has been has sometimes been towards relaxing legal enforcement, eg the greater ease of obtaining exemption orders for women to work at nights. The intrusion of the law has been through the indirect effects of other legislation, eg the Employment Protection Act or the Equal Pay Act. This trend is likely to continue unless there is some change in the practice of Government.

CHAPTER 9

❡❡❡❡❡❡❡❡❡❡❡❡

Summary and conclusions

THE CHANGING PATTERNS IN HOURS OF WORK

In the USA the 35 or 36 hour week is common with industrial workers and the 32 hour week is by no means unknown. Many UK office workers have a working week of between 35 to 40 hours and men and women on shift systems with a paid meal break work $37\frac{1}{2}$ hours a week. A general reduction in the hours of work of industrial workers in this country cannot be very far away. It may take place as a means of reducing high unemployment, if this proves to be of a long term structural nature and not the short term effects of temporary economic difficulties. Few have suggested that Britain's economic plight is due to the length of the working week, as distinct from how effectively the time at work is used; indeed the charge has been made more frequently that industrial workers with large amounts of overtime are working too long and although the amount of overtime has declined in recent years it is still considerable. Regular overtime working can lead to low productivity and overmanning. When the hours of work are reduced further, it seems unlikely that manufacturers will find it economic to work their plant for 36 hours a week and some extension of shiftworking seems inevitable.

The 40 hour week has led to many novel changes in the

arrangement of hours including flexible working hours, the compressed week, 12 hour shifts on three shift work. As the hours of work are reduced further other arrangements will be adopted. Fleuter (1975) in a book entitled *The Work Week Revolution* cites examples of the 35 hour five shift week in the USA. He continues by giving examples of two groups of operators manning a computer plant over a six day week, each group working three 12 hour shifts. He goes on to speculate on the working of a 'continuous' week where two crews work three and a half 10 hour shifts, so keeping the factory or office working seven days a week. Another arrangement would be to work three 10 hour shifts one week and four the next. These solutions adopt a day shift extending over six or seven days of the week manned by two crews, but the conventional solution adopted in this country has been the working of a double day shift or an alternating day/night shift. The latter has been extensively worked in some industries, although the double day shift is an alternative which involves less stress on the shiftworker for there is no nightwork and is more common in other European countries. It is probable that in the medium to long term there will be an extension of two shiftworking in one form or another which will involve larger numbers of men and women than at present. Service industries are also continuing to increase in size and many of them involve shiftwork. Three shiftworking will increase with the continued growth in the capital costs of plant and equipment in many industries, but this may not lead to an increase in the numbers of shiftworkers for capital intensive industries are not usually labour intensive. Whatever the movement in numbers there will be much greater variety and flexibility in working hours.

Another alteration in the habits of work and rest is the change in the pattern of meal breaks. The main lunch break during the day is becoming shorter and the tendency is to eat a light meal or a snack rather than a cooked meal. For office workers and manual workers on light work a half hour lunch break with sandwiches or salad provides enough rest and refreshment and is a practice which meets the recommendations of doctors and dieticians who highlight the modern vice of overeating. The shortening of the lunch break has its effect on the distribution of working hours.

Changes in the arrangement of working hours have been a feature of the last two decades. A continuation of this together with a further shortening of the weekly hours is likely to be a feature of the next two decades. It is surprising how quickly old established patterns and habits have been upset. It is only 10 years since, in 1967, flexible working hours or 'gliding' time was first introduced in an organized scheme in a West German engineering firm. The changes in the arrangement of shifts have not been so revolutionary, but there is no doubt that they will occur at an ever increasing rate and it is important to make the choices which are suitable for the local situation.

Shiftwork and management

Management should make a thorough economic assessment of the length of time it requires to utilize plant; in doing so it should take into account present utilization of plant and work-people, size of the market and the likely level of demand and a rigorous costing of the alternative shift systems. Management will have to pay due regard to manpower factors such as the availability of labour, the adequacy of supervisory and management staff and the location of the plant. Labour costs will be the largest current expenditure increase as the result of introducing shiftwork.

The next step is to enter into consultation with representatives of the employees in a two stage process. The first is concerned with introducing a shift system and the second is the maintenance of a system already operating. Consultation at a very early stage is vital to win acceptance for the introduction of shiftwork which is more likely if the need for it is apparent to all. Consultation may then move into the negotiating and bargaining stage over the compensation for working shifts, including the premia and possibly the shortening of the weekly hours of work. There are often choices of which shift system to adopt, the type of rota, the length of the shifts, the starting and stopping times, the timing and duration of the breaks, etc. Some of these are predetermined by the nature of the work or economic considerations but many can be freely decided with reference to local custom, shiftworkers' preferences, the need to provide adequate spells for rest and leisure, keeping as many weekends as possible free from duty, etc. Scientists are carrying out research which may lead to recommendations on the optimum arrangement for shift hours but no very firm guidelines are yet available. One of the desirable features of any rota system is that it should be simple and easy to understand so that the shiftworker may plan his leisure. The employees need the new system explained to them as well as being kept informed of the progress of negotiations. The next step is to plan the introduction of the system which may be more easily done in stages; the size of the crews have to be determined, the provision of adequate supervision and the training of staff. The numbers and skills of shift support and maintenance staff are important to get right if interruptions to the work flow are to be avoided.

The legal requirements have to be checked. They relate primarily to restrictions in the hours of work for women and young persons. But there are also requirements relating to the provision of medical and first aid services, and safety and health requirements which may have to be provided for dangerous or unhealthy processes. General welfare cover has to be arranged so that the shiftworkers are not at too great a disadvantage compared to day-workers. These should include welfare arrangements for catering and facilities for eating meals, points of reference for welfare and pay queries, provision for holiday and emergency cover at work and any special transport and parking facilities which may have to be arranged for shiftworkers.

In maintaining a shift system, particularly when night-work is involved, it is important to see that the workers do not become isolated from the day-time life of the factory. There is a tendency for shiftworkers to form closely integrated groups perhaps with a touch of defensiveness. It is up to management to see that there is effective two way communication between the shift-workers and day-time staff. Shift crews may also experience communication difficulties between themselves which can sometimes lead to tension. Managers will need to spend some time in the factory at night to check, among other things, on the adequacy of supervision but perhaps most important just to be seen on the shop floor. Shift supervisors should meet together as a group from time to time. Both managers and supervisors need adequate remuneration for working unsocial hours and for any extra duties which they may have to discharge. If a shift system is carefully installed and maintained there is no reason why productivity at night and in the evening should not be as high or nearly as high as on the day shift.

Shiftwork and employee

To the employee, working on shifts affects all aspects of his life. The increased earnings enable him and his family to enjoy a higher standard of living and this is the single most important inducement which encourages him to work on shifts. The importance of higher wages can be exaggerated and account has to be taken of the non-financial costs which the shiftworker pays. The problems are most accute where nightwork is involved. The shiftworker and his manager should be informed about the hygiene of shiftwork, so that they have an understanding of the effects of shiftwork on bodily processes. They should be aware of the disturbance to bodily rhythms and the effects these will have on alertness at different times during the night: the need to consider the introduction of rest pauses or a change of activity where the work is demanding in terms of attention or excessively boring.

Shiftworkers can be reassured that nightwork is unlikely to have long term adverse effects on their health but if they have a predisposition to gastro-intestinal complaints or nervous disorders, then they need to take special care to see that they get enough sleep, have a balanced diet and attend to habits of elimination. If shiftwork is still unduly stressful then they might reconsider the wisdom of working at night. If they have symptoms they should see their doctor and discuss the problem with him. Bodily discomfort is the lot of many nightworkers and not enough recognition is given to this in planning and monitoring nightwork. Some people do not adapt at all well to it and even when they have had time to adjust they fail to do so. Others after some years on shiftwork or those who are getting on in years find the strain of shiftwork increases. It is most desirable that these people should be able to transfer to daywork although they sacrifice the shiftwork premia. Some kind of safety net is required for shiftworkers so that they do not become trapped in a situation which might result in impairment to health. Most shiftworkers who work nights do reach some kind of physical adjustment and become adapted to a system they have worked on for a time.

The other main effects of shiftwork on an employee are on his social and domestic life. These apply to day shift systems when work is carried out in the evenings as well as systems where nightwork is involved. There are differences between the social and physical effects of shiftwork in that none of the latter are beneficial in any respect, they are all adverse; while shiftwork has compensating advantages in social and domestic life. If a shiftworker develops leisure interests which are family centred or involve activities during the day which are flexible in the times they can be carried out, then he may enjoy these advantages of shiftwork but if he wishes to pursue organized community activities the times of which are inflexible, then he will be disappointed and will not be able to take a full part in them. This is more important at some ages and in stages of family development than at others. The young single shiftworker is intolerant of the afternoon and night shifts as they interfere with his social life but to the family man the disadvantages may not be so great. If the shiftworker has heavy responsibilities with financial commitment then extra earnings are important to him. This is one reason why more family men with young children and heavy domestic responsibilities, in their middle years, tend to work shifts more frequently than either younger or older men. Shiftworkers also seem able to keep up with the extended family and friends quite well. Nevertheless the social and domestic compensations to shiftwork must not be overstated for there are disadvantages both to the shiftworker and his wife, who may dislike her husband's working hours and feel anxious in the evening and at night when she is left alone in the house. There is a real impairment of social and
196

domestic roles although the extent of the latter awaits further research.

SHIFTWORK AND RESEARCH

Quite a lot of basic research has been carried out on physiological disturbance caused by shiftwork and its effect on health. There is a forum for scientists engaged in this field in the periodic conferences organized by the sub-committee on shiftwork of the Permanent Commission and International Association on Occupational Health. Experimental physiologists and psychologists are gaining fresh insights into the effects of changed time schedules and disturbance to circadian rhythms on performance, the quantity and quality of day time sleep and the ability to adapt to the 'inversion' of night and day. In time this work will provide guidelines for arranging shift rotas, particularly the length of the spells of work at night and the frequency of changing shifts. It is always possible to argue for more research but in this area progress has been made.

In the areas of the social and domestic consequences of shiftwork and the wider sociological implications to the community, research has not been so extensive. There is room for more research to investigate in greater detail the social consequences of different types of shiftwork, for results could suggest remedial action and provide guidance to shiftworkers. The effects of shiftwork on communities has usually been carried out incidentally when examining some other problem. Intensive investigation of shiftworkers' time budgets are overdue, as they would give information on how people on different shifts spend their time during their periods of rest and relaxation and what effect this is likely to have on the wider activities of the community. If shiftwork becomes even more extensively worked data from time budgets

197

will be required for planning purposes. Already the operation of flexible working hours has altered the distribution of times people journey to and from work, as office workers on flexitime are inclined to get to work earlier than the normal starting time. The social consequences of changes in the length and pattern of working hours need careful monitoring.

There are large gaps in our knowledge about shift-working and practical applications, where a small investment in research and development would yield an immediate return. Three such areas are:

the monitoring of changes in current practice
the preparation of guidelines on the hygiene of shift-work
the examination of individual differences in adjustment to nightwork.

The many changes in current practice in the arrangement of hours of work and particularly shiftwork have been discussed. These changes in working hours have not come about in response to research findings but as a result of management and work-people adapting shift systems to suit local conditions and employees' preferences. There are two excellent examples of what can be done to monitor these changes, in the work of Sloane (1975b) who investigated changing patterns of working hours and in the periodic surveys of shiftwork by the Industrial Society (1975). The Advisory Conciliation and Arbitration Service (ACAS) is also available for management or workers to turn to for advice. It has built up a series of case studies to which it can refer. Incomes Data Services, the British Institute of Management (BIM) and the Department of Employment monitor changes in shift-workers, earnings and premia. Managers and personnel officers exchange experiences. Nevertheless there is little systematic monitoring of current trends which if carried out could provide useful guidance to firms contemplating a change. The information obtained would be concerned with the conditions which are conducive to change, the causes of failure and pitfalls to avoid and the reasons for success and how to build on them. The monitoring of change and feedback as to its consequences is an essential step in successful development.

A simple guide to the shiftworker on the hygiene of shiftwork would be invaluable. It should be possible to prepare one or more short pamphlets explaining the effects of shiftwork on bodily processes, circadian rhythms, sleep, digestion, etc. This could be complemented by advice on diet, sleeping and attention to personal habits, etc. Such guidance could be given in conjunction with a lecture and discussion prior to an employee taking up nightwork for the first time.

Wide individual differences in people's ability to adjust to night work has been noted. Some people never adjust, others do so with difficulty and live under some stress, yet others are relatively unaffected by shiftwork. There is a suggestion that it is the 'evening type' – the person alert later in the day – who adjusts better than the 'morning type' and a lead such as this should be explored further. Failure to adjust may be due to disturbance to bodily rhythms or to psychological difficulties of adjusting to changed family and social circumstances. There is scope for physiologists and psychologists together to discover the reasons why some people adjust and others do not. In time they might develop tests which would reveal individual differences and enable advice to be given on the suitability of a person for nightwork.

SHIFTWORK AND COMMUNITY

Extensive use of shiftwork with between a fifth and a third of men in manufacturing industry working unusual hours has an effect on the community. Two changes are:

in the role of the family
in the use of leisure.

Young and Willmot (1973) in their study of work and leisure in the London region point to the growth of the symmetrical family. In this type of family organization husbands' and wives' roles are joint rather than segregated and in the small nuclear family they share the major activities of the household. The husband takes on tasks, not only those which are traditionally men's, but even clothes' washing or bed making and he shares in the rearing of children. Leisure interests are also pursued together and the husband takes his family with him when he goes out for social activity and recreation. This trend was very noticeable and increasing among the families surveyed by Young and Willmott; although unisex has not yet arrived! There are many reasons for this change outside the scope of the present argument but it is notable that this symmetrical pattern of family life is one which is reinforced by shiftwork. However Young and Willmott came to the opposite conclusion and wrote:

fathers are forced to work when other members of their family are at leisure and to take their leisure when other members are at work. The life of the family can hardly be enhanced, even though the motive is to enhance the means for its support.

This is true when both the husband and wife work full time. But if the family is in the phase of expansion with young children and the wife stays at home to look after them, then the shiftworker and his wife can share the husband's free time; including in their activities the children when they are of pre-school age or in the school holidays.

We have noted in the chapter on *Effects on social and family life* that the shiftworker's interests are home centred to a greater extent than with other people. An advantage to his wife of having a husband on shifts is that he is available for companionship during the week, he can help with housework and shopping and he may take her and the family out. In many instances the results of working shifts are that the shiftworker and his family are pushed into shared activities, sometimes to the exclusion of other interests, which reinforce the growth of the symmetrical family. This could be the single most important consequence of shiftwork for the community.

THE NEED FOR FLEXIBILITY

An underlying theme of this book has been the need for flexibility. Generalizations about shiftwork are out of place. The variety of shift systems and arrangements of hours are too great and people's responses to them are so different. Many of the changes have either been at the instigation of management with a view to improving the welfare of employees or in response to pressure from a group of staff for change. The changes have been made to meet group needs but there is now an attempt to meet individual needs in the arrangement of working hours. The increased complexity and variety of working hours has led to an element of choice. This is in agreement with the widespread effort to allow individuals and small groups more autonomy over the way they organize their work and the methods by which they carry it out. The motto we might bear in mind when considering the human aspects of shiftwork is that *People Matter* and *People Differ*.

Bibliography

⟣⟣⟣⟣⟣⟣⟣⟣⟣⟣⟣⟣⟣⟣⟣⟣

AANONSEN A, *Shiftwork and Health,* Scandinavian University Books, Oslo, 1964

ADVISORY, CONCILIATION AND ARBITRATION SERVICE, *Shiftworking – Some Problem Areas*, Unpublished Report, 1976

ALDEN J, *Two Jobs or One? New Society*, 37, 660, 1976a

ALDEN J, The Extent and Nature of Double Jobbing in Great Britain. Unpublished Report, 1976b

ALLUSI E A, Influence of Work/Rest Scheduling and Sleep Loss on Sustained Performance. In *Aspects of Human Efficiency,* (ed Colquhoun W P), The English Universities Press, London, 1972

ANDLAUER P and FOURRÉ L, *Aspects Ergonomiques du Travail en Equipes Alternatives,* Centre d'Etudes de Physiologie Appliquée au Travail, Strasbourg, 1962

BANKS O, Continuous Shiftwork: The Attitudes of Wives, *Occupational Psychology,* 30, 69–84, 1956

BANKS O, *The Attitudes of Steelworkers to Technical Change,* Liverpool University Press, 1960

BIENEFELD M A, *Working Hours in British Industry,* London School of Economics and Political Science, Weidenfeld and Nicolson, London, 1972

BJERNER B, HOLM A and SVENSSON A, Diurnal Variation in Mental Performance: A Study of three Shiftworkers, *British Journal of Industrial Medicine*, 12, 103–110, 1955

BLAKE M J F, Temperament and Time of Day, in *Biological Rhythms and Human Performance*, (ed Colquhoun W P) Academic Press, London, 1971

BLAKELOCK E, A New Look at the New Leisure, *Administrative Science Quarterly,* 4, 446–467, 1960

202

BRITISH INSTITUTE OF MANAGEMENT, *Shiftwork,* Information Summary 119, London, 1965

BRITISH INSTITUTE OF MANAGEMENT, *Computer Staff Shiftwork,* London, 1968

BROWN D, Shiftwork: A Survey of the Sociological Implications of Studies of Male Shiftworkers, *Journal of Occupational Psychology,* 48, 231–240, 1975

BROWN H G, *Some Effects of Shiftwork on Social and Domestic Life,* Yorkshire Bulletin of Economic and Social Research, Occasional Paper No 2, Hull, 1959

BROWNE R C, The Day and Night Performance of Teleprinter Switchboard Operators, *Occupational Psychology,* 23, 121–126, 1949

BULLOCK N, DICKENS P, SHAPCOTT M and STEADMAN P, Time Budgets and Models of Urban Activity Patterns, *Social Trends,* No 5, 45–63, HMSO, London, 1974

CAILLOT R, Conséquences Sociales du Travail à feu continu, *Economie et Humanisme,* 122, 62–72, 1959

CHADWICK–JONES J K, *Automation and Behaviour,* John Wiley, London, 1969

CHURCHILL D, Four Day 40 Hours, Industrial Society, November/December, 16–18, 1975

COLQUHOUN W P, BLAKE M J F and EDWARDS R S, Experimental Studies of Shiftwork, I. A Comparison of 'Rotating' and 'Stabilized' Four Hour Shift Systems, *Ergonomics,* 11, 437–453, 1968a

COLQUHOUN W P, BLAKE M J F and EDWARDS R S, Experimental Studies of Shiftwork, II. Stabilized Eight Hour Shift Systems, *Ergonomics,* 11, 527–546, 1968b

COLQUHOUN W P, BLAKE M J F and EDWARDS R S, Experimental Studies of Shiftwork, III. Stabilized 12 Hour Shift Systems, *Ergonomics,* 12, 865–882, 1969

COLQUHOUN W P, Circadian Variations in Mental Efficiency, In *Biological Rhythms and Human Performance,* (ed Colquhoun W P), Academic Press, London, 1971

CONFEDERATION OF BRITISH INDUSTRY, *Shiftwork: Differential Rates of Payment and Allowances for Shiftwork or Night Work,* London, 1976

Conroy R T W L and Mill S J N, *Human Circadian Rhythms*, Churchill, London, 1970

De La Mare G and Shimmin S, Preferred Patterns of Duty in a Flexible Shiftworking Situation, *Occupational Psychology*, 38, 203–214, 1964

De La Mare G and Walker J, Shiftworking: the Arrangement of Hours on Night Work, *Nature*, 208, 1127–1128, 1965

De La Mare G and Walker J, Factors Influencing the Choice of Shift Rotation, *Occupational Psychology*, 42, 1–21, 1968

Department of Employment, *Time Rates of Wages and Hours of Work*, HMSO, London, 1976

Department of Employment and Productivity, *Hours of Employment of Women and Young Persons Employed in Factories*, HMSO, London, 1969

Dirken J M, Industrial Shiftwork: Decrease in Well-being and Specific Effects, *Ergonomics*, 9, 115–124, 1966

Doll R, Jones A and Buckatzsch M M, *Occupational Factors in the Aetiology of Gastric and Duodenal Ulcers*, Medical Research Council Special Report, No 276, HMSO, London, 1951

Downie J H, *Some Social and Industrial Implications of Shiftwork*, Industrial Welfare Society, London, 1963

Drenth P J D, Hoolwerf G and Thierry H, Psychological Aspects of Shiftwork, from *Personal Goals and Work Design* (ed Warr P) John Wiley, London, 1976

Fishwick F and Harling G J, *Shiftworking in the Motor Industry*, National Economic Development Office, London, 1974

Fleuter D L, *The Work Week Revolution*, Addison-Wesley Publishing Company, Reading, Massachusetts, 1975

Health of Munitions Workers Committee, *Industrial Efficiency and Fatigue*, Interim Report, CD 85111, HMSO, London, 1917

Health of Munitions Workers Committee, *Industrial Health and Efficiency*, Final Report, CD 9065, HMSO, London, 1918

Health and Safety Executive, *Hours of Employment of Women and Young Persons*, Health and Safety at Work Booklet, No 23, HMSO, London, 1975
204

HEDGES J N, New Patterns for Working Time, *Monthly Labour Review*, February, 4–8, 1973

HOME DEPARTMENT, *Report of a Departmental Committee on the Employment of Women and Young Persons on the Two Shift System*, Cmnd 4914, HMSO, London, 1935

HUGHES D G and FOLKARD S, Adaptation to an Eight Hour Shift in Living Routine by Members of a Socially Isolated Community, *Nature*, 264, 432–434, 1976.

INCOMES DATA SERVICES, *Shiftwork Study*, No 44, No 48 and No 65: 1973: Study No 110, London, 1975

INDUSTRIAL SOCIETY, *Survey of Shiftworking Practices*, Survey No 194, London, 1975

INDUSTRIAL WELFARE SOCIETY, *Shiftwork in Offices*, Information Survey and Report Series, No 126, London, 1965

JONES B J, *The Economic Aspects of Shiftwork*, Industrial Welfare Society, Information Survey and Report Series, No 112, London, 1963

KLEITMAN N, *Sleep and Wakefulness*, University of Chicago Press, Chicago, 1963

KNAUTH P and RUTENFRANZ J, The Effects of Noise on the Sleep of Night Workers, In *Experimental Studies of Shiftwork*, (ed Colquhoun P, *et al*) Westdeutscher Verlag, 1975

KOGI H, TAKAHASHI M and ONISHI N, Experimental Evaluation of Frequent Eight-Hour versus Less Frequent Longer Night Shifts, In *Experimental Studies of Shiftwork*, (eds Colquhoun P and Folkard S), Proceedings of the Third International Symposium on Night and Shiftwork, Westdeutscher Verlag, 1975

LAMBERT L and HART S, Who Needs a Father? *New Society*, 37, 80, 1976

LIPSET S M, TROW M and COLEMAN J, *Union Democracy*, Double Day Anchor, New York, 1956

LOBBAN M C, The Entrainment of Circadian Rhythms in Man, In *Cold Spring Harbor — Symposium on Quantitative Biology*, Cold Spring Harbor Laboratory of Quantitative Biology, 25, 325–332, 1960

MARRIS R L, *The Economics of Capital Utilization: A Report on Multiple Shiftwork*, Cambridge University Press, 1964

MARRIS R L, The Economics of Shiftworking, In *The Benefits and Problems of Shiftworking,* Production Engineering Research Association of Great Britain, 1966

MARRIS R L, *Multiple Shiftwork,* National Economic Development Office, HMSO, London, 1970

MANN F C and HOFFMAN L R, *Automation and the Worker,* Henry Holt, New York, 1960

MAURICE M, *Shift Work,* International Labour Office, Geneva, 1975

MEERS A, Performance on Different Turn of Duty Within a Three Shift System and its Relation to Body Temperature, In *Experimental Studies of Shiftwork*, (ed Colquhoun P *et al*), Westdeutscher Verlag, Germany, 1975

MENZEL W, *Menschliche Tag – Nacht – Rhythmik und Schichtarbeit,* Benno Schwabe, Basel/Stuttgart, 1962

MINISTRY OF LABOUR, Shiftworking, Ministry of Labour Gazette, 73, 148–155, 1965

MINISTRY OF LABOUR, *Introduction of Shiftworking,* HMSO, London, 1967

MINISTRY OF LABOUR AND NATIONAL SERVICE, *Report of a Committee on Double Day Shiftworking*, Cmnd 7147, HMSO, London, 1947

MOTT P E, MANN F C, McLOUGHLIN Q and WARWICK D P, *Shiftwork*, University of Michigan Press, Ann Arbor, 1965

MURRELL K F H, *Ergonomics,* Chapman and Hall, 1965

NACHREINER F, Role Perceptions, Job Satisfaction and Attitudes towards Shiftwork of Workers in Different Shift Systems as Related to Situational and Personal Factors, In *Experimental Studies in Shiftwork* (ed Colquhoun P, *et al*) Westdeutscher Verlag, 1975

NATIONAL BOARD FOR PRICES AND INCOMES, *Hours of Work, Overtime and Shiftworking,* Report No 161, Cmnd 4554 and Supplement Cmnd 4554 1, HMSO, London, 1970

OATLEY K and GOODWIN B C, The Explanation and Investigation of Biological Rhythms, In *Biological Rhythms and Human Performance* (ed Colquhoun W P) Academic Press, London, 1971

OSTBERG O, Inter-Individual Differences in Circadian Fatigue Patterns of Shiftworkers, *British Journal of Industrial Medicine,* 30, 341–351, 1973

OSTBERG O and SVENSSON G, 'Functional Age' and Physical Work Capacity during the Day and Night, In *Experimental Studies of Shiftwork*, (ed Colquhoun P, *et al*), Westdeutscher Verlag, Germany, 1975

PATKAI P, PETTERSSON K and ÅKERSTEDT T, The Diurnal Pattern of some Physiological and Psychological Functions in Permanent Night Workers and in Men Working on a Two-Shift (day and night) System, in *Experimental Studies of Shiftwork*, (eds Colquhoun P and Folkard S). Proceedings of the Third International Symposium on Night and Shiftwork, Westdeutscher Verlag, 1975

POCOCK S J, SERGEAN R and TAYLOR P J, Absence of Continuous Three Shift Workers, *Occupational Psychology*, 46, 7–13, 1972

POOR R, *Four Days, 40 Hours,* Bursk and Poor Publishing, Cambridge, Massachusetts, 1970

POWELL D C, *How to Plan a Shift Rota,* Industrial Society, London, 1966

RAY J T, MARTIN O and ALLUSI E A, *Human Performance as a Function of the Work/Rest Cycle*, National Academy of Sciences, National Research Council, Washington, 1961

RUTENFRANZ J, KNAUTH P and COLQUHOUN W P, Hours of Work and Shiftwork, *Ergonomics*, 19, 331–340, 1976

SALAMON G, *Community and Occupation,* Cambridge University Press, 1974

SERGEAN R, *Managing Shiftwork,* Gower Press and Industrial Society, London, 1971

SERGEAN R, HOWELL D, TAYLOR P J and POCOCK S J, Compensation for Inconvenience: An Analysis of Shift Payments in Collective Agreements in the UK, *Occupational Psychology*, 43, 183–192, 1969

SHEPHERD R D and WALKER J, Three Shift Working and the Distribution of Absence, *Occupational Psychology*, 30, 105–111, 1956

SLOANE P J, Flexible Working Hours, *Department of Employment Gazette*, 83, 3–5, 1975a

SLOANE P J, *Changing Patterns of Working Hours*, Department of Employment Manpower Paper No 13, HMSO, London, 1975b

SMITH M and VERNON M D, The Two Shift System in Certain Factories, in *Two Studies on Hours of Work*, Industrial Fatigue Research Board, Report No 43, HMSO, London, 1928

TAYLOR P J, Shift and Day Work, A Comparison of Sickness Absence, Lateness and other Absence Behaviour in an Oil Refinery from 1962 to 1965, *British Journal of Industrial Medicine*, 24, 93–102, 1967

TAYLOR P J, Personal Factors Associated with Sickness Absence, A study of 194 Men with Contrasting Sickness Absence Experience in a Refinery Population, *British Journal of Industrial Medicine*, 25, 106–118, 1968

TAYLOR P J and POCOCK S J, Mortality of Shift and Day Workers, 1956 – 1968, *British Journal of Industrial Medicine*, 29, 201–207, 1972

TAYLOR P J, POCOCK S J and SERGEAN R, Absenteeism of Shift and Day Workers, *British Journal of Industrial Medicine*, 29, 208–213, 1972

THIIS-EVANSEN E, Shiftwork and Health, *Industrial Medicine and Surgery*, 27, 493–497, 1948

THIIS–EVANSEN E, Shiftwork and Health, In *On Night and Shiftwork*, (ed Svensson A), Studia Laboris et Salutis, National Institute of Occupational Health, Stockholm, 1970

TRADES UNION CONGRESS, *Overtime and Shiftworking: A Guide for Negotiators*, London, 1973

TUNE G S, Sleep and Wakefulness in a Group of Shiftworkers, *British Journal of Industrial Medicine*, 26, 54–58, 1969

VAN LOON J H, Diurnal Body Temperature Curves in Shiftworkers, *Ergonomics*, 6, 267–273, 1963

VERNON H M, *The Health and Efficiency of Munition Workers*, Oxford University Press, 1940

VROOM V H, *Work and Motivation*, John Wiley and Sons, London, 1964

WALKER J, Shift Changes and Hours of Work, *Occupational Psychology,* 35, 1–9, 1961

WALKER J, Frequent Alternation of Shifts on Continuous Work, *Occupational Psychology,* 40, 215–225, 1966

WALKER J and DE LA MARE G, Absence from Work in Relation to Length and Distribution of Shift Hours, *British Journal of Industrial Medicine,* 28, 36–44, 1971

WEDDERBURN A A I, Social Factors in Satisfaction with Swiftly Rotating Shifts, Occupational Psychology, 41, 85–107, 1967

WEDDERBURN A A I, EEG and Self-Recorded Sleep of Two Shiftworkers over Four Weeks of Real and Synthetic Work, In *Experimental Studies of Shiftwork,* (ed Colquhoun P *et al*) Westdeutscher Verlag, 1975a

WEDDERBURN A A I, *Studies of Shiftwork in the Steel Industry,* Department of Business Organization, Heriot-Watt University, 1975b

WHEELER H E, *The Four Day Week: an AMA Research Report,* American Management Association, New York, 1972

WILKINSON R T, Effects of up to 60 Hours' Sleep Deprivation on Different Types of Work, *Ergonomics,* 7, 175–186, 1964

WILKINSON R T, Hours of Work and the Twenty Four Hour Cycle of Rest and Activity, In *Psychology at Work,* (ed Warr P B) Penguin Books, 1971

WINDLE E, HODGSON C and LOGAN K, *Shiftwork in Dunlop,* The Dunlop Company, 1969

WYATT S and MARRIOTT R, Night Work and Shift Changes, *British Journal of Industrial Medicine,* 10, 164–172, 1953

YOUNG J and WILLMOTT P, *The Symmetrical Family,* Routledge and Kegan Paul, London, 1973

INDEX

oooooooooo